Chinese Characters for HSK: Level 5

Sheldon Smith

Chinese Characters for HSK: Level 5

ISBN: 978-1-912579-95-2

First Edition

This book is published by Evident Press. For more information on this title and others in the Chinese Character for HSK series, visit www.evidentpress.com.

About the author
Sheldon Smith was born in Singapore but grew up in England. He has lived and worked in China since 2002. He currently resides in Guangzhou, Guangdong province. In addition to text books for learning Chinese he is the author of several novels and text books for academic English (the *EAP Foundation* series).

Additional Learning Resouces
All books publiushed by Evdent Press include access to free additional online resources. To access the resources you will need to use a code. The code for *ChineseCharacters for HSK: Level 5* is **printed at the back of the book, following the final character (醉).** To use this code and access the resources, please visit www.evidentpress.com/resources/.

Contents

Preface

This is the third book in the HSK Characters series of text books. It covers characters used in Level 5 of the HSK (Hanyu Shuiping Kaoshi) test.

Key features of the book
The following are some of the key features of the book.

- It covers all *new* characters in level 5 of the HSK test (621 in total), using the simplified characters of modern standard Chinese.
- It includes all HSK words which use those characters, up to level 6 (1531 words in total, comprising 749 in level 5 and 782 in level 6).
- The level of each word is given, so you can choose which to study.
- Alongside each character is its pronunciation and meaning. If a character has more than one pronunciation in the test, each is given.
- The radical and number of strokes is also given for each character.
- Characters are arranged alphabetically for easy identification.
- There are notes for some characters to give additional information.
- There are some level 5 words which use only characters introduced in levels 1 to 4. These are included as an appendix. There are 551 such words, which, together with the 749 words in the characters pages totals 1300, the number of new words in level 5.
- Additional words, outside of the HSK list, are included for many of the characters, to allow for vocabulary expansion.
- A 'double entry' system is used for each word, meaning it is listed under *all* characters which appear in that word.
- Additional appendices give information on measure words and radicals*.
- Indexes at the end allow you to find characters according to their English meaning and radical*.

* The appendix on radicals and the radical index is available in the Kindle version only.

Why learn characters?
There are three main reasons to learn Chinese characters rather than focusing purely on words. First, characters are the building blocks of Chinese. Most Chinese words consist of two characters in combination, each of which conveys meaning. Knowing the characters and their meaning makes it much easier to learn the word. Second, it is easier to learn new words if they are themed or connected in some way. Studying characters will allow you to learn words which share that character, which should make the words easier to learn than if they are studied in isolation. The final reason for learning characters relates to 'economies of scale'. The HSK test in total comprises 5000 words across 6 levels. However, there are only 2663 characters, or around half as many.

Who is the book for?

The book covers level 5 characters, and is therefore suitable for learners who have progressed from level 4. At the same time, more than half of the words using level 5 characters are level 6 words, so this book will also enable learners to get a head start on the final level of the HSK test.

About the HSK test: Level 5

The Hanyu Shuiping Kaoshi (汉语水平考试), or HSK for short, is China's only standardised test of the Chinese language. It is designed for non-native speakers, such as foreign students and overseas Chinese, and approximates to the English TOEFL or IELTS test. An HSK certificate can be used throughout China as evidence of language proficiency for higher education and work.

Level 5 of the test is designed for learners who can read Chinese newspapers and magazines, understand Chinese films and TV, and can write and deliver a full speech in Chinese. There are 2500 total words in level 5, comprising 1300 new words together with the 1200 words introduced in levels 1 to 4. Altogether the words in level 5 use 1685 characters, with 621 new characters to go along with the 1064 characters introduced in levels 1 to 4. To put it differently, there are fewer total characters than words in level 5 (1685 vs 2500, about *two thirds* as many), and also fewer new characters than new words (621 vs 1300, or fewer than *half* as many). This potentially reduces the amount of learning required to master words in the HSK level 5. This book covers those 621 new characters.

Guide to the characters pages

The diagram below explains the information on the characters pages.

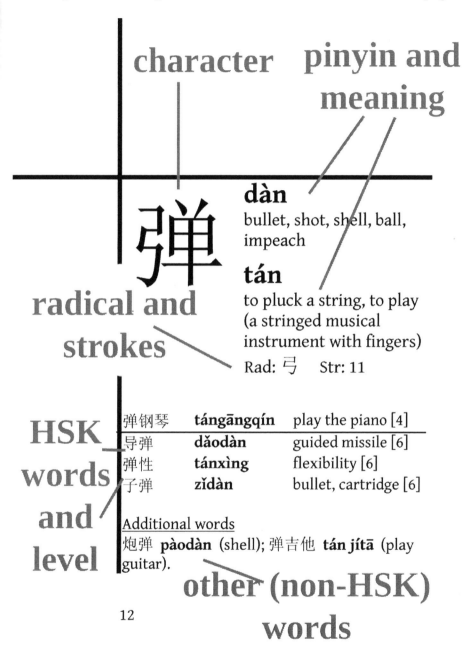

character

pinyin and meaning

dàn
bullet, shot, shell, ball, impeach

tán
to pluck a string, to play (a stringed musical instrument with fingers)

Rad: 弓　　Str: 11

radical and strokes

HSK words and level

弹钢琴	**tángāngqín**	play the piano [4]
导弹	**dǎodàn**	guided missile [6]
弹性	**tánxìng**	flexibility [6]
子弹	**zǐdàn**	bullet, cartridge [6]

Additional words
炮弹 **pàodàn** (shell); 弹吉他 **tán jítā** (play guitar).

other (non-HSK) words

12

āi
hey (interjection)

Rad: 口   Str: 8

哎   **āi**   hey, look out, why (interjection) [5]

ài
yes, oh, right (interjection)

Rad: 口   Str: 10

唉   **āi**   to express realisation or agreement (yes, oh, right etc.) [5]

ài
to hinder, to obstruct, to block

Rad: 石   Str: 13

妨碍	**fáng'ài**	hinder, hamper, obstruct, impede, make difficult [5]
障碍	**zhàng'ài**	barrier, obstacle, hinder, block, obstruct [6]
阻碍	**zǔ'ài**	impede, hinder, block, obstacle, hindrance [6]

àn
bank, shore, beach, coast

Rad: 山   Str: 8

岸   **àn**   bank, shore, coast [5]

Additional words
堤岸 **dī'àn** (embankment).

1

暗 àn

dark, gloomy, hidden, secret, to shut the door, unilluminated

Rad: 日   Str: 13

| 暗 | àn | dark, secret, hidden, gloomy [5] |
| 暗示 | ànshì | to hint, to suggest, suggestion, a hint [6] |

Additional words
暗暗 **ànàn** (secretly); 黑暗 **hēi'àn** (dark).

熬 áo

to boil, stew, to simmer, endure

Rad: 灬   Str: 14

| 熬夜 | áoyè | stay up late [5] |
| 熬 | áo | boil for a long time (when cooking), endure, suffer [6] |

巴 bā

tail, suffix for certain nouns, to hope, to wish

Rad: 巴   Str: 4

尾巴	wěiba	tail [5]
巴不得	bābude	anxious, look forward to [6]
巴结	bājie	to fawn on, to curry favour with, to suck up to [6]

Additional words
淋巴结 **lín bā jié** (lymph gland);
翘尾巴 **qiào wěiba** (to be cocky, be snobbish and self-important (lit. to hold up the tail));
嘴巴 **zuǐbā** (mouth).

摆 bǎi

pendulum, to swing, to oscillate, to show, to move, to exhibit

Rad: 扌   Str: 13

摆	bǎi	pendulum, move to and fro, sway, arrange, exhibit [5]
摆脱	bǎituō	free oneself from, get rid of [6]
摇摆	yáobǎi	sway, swing, rock, wigwag, vacillate [6]

Additional words
摇摆舞 **yáobǎiwǔ** (rock 'n' roll).

bǎn
a register, a block of printing, an edition, version, page

Rad: 片　Str: 8

出版	**chūbǎn**	publish [5]
版本	**bǎnběn**	edition, version [6]

伴

bàn
a partner, companion or associate, to accompany, comrade

Rad: 亻　Str: 7

伙伴	**huǒbàn**	fellow, partner, mate, pal, friend [5]
伴侣	**bànlǚ**	companion, mate, partner [6]
伴随	**bànsuí**	to go with, accompany [6]

bǎng
upper arm, wing, to flirt, puffed (swollen), bladder

Rad: 月　Str: 14

翅膀	**chìbǎng**	wing [5]
肩膀	**jiānbǎng**	shoulder [5]

bàng
near (approaching)

Rad: 亻　Str: 12

傍晚	**bàngwǎn**	toward evening, at nightfall [5]

báo
mean, slight, thin, meagre, small, ungenerous, unkind

bó
weak

Rad: 卄   Str: 16

薄	**báo**	thin, cold in manner, indifferent [5]
薄弱	**bóruò**	weak, frail [6]

bǎo
a jewel, a gem, a treasure, precious

Rad: 宀   Str: 8

宝贝	**bǎobèi**	precious thing, treasured object, darling [5]
宝贵	**bǎoguì**	valuable, precious [5]

Additional words
宝剑 **bǎojiàn** (double-edged sword).

bēi
sad, sadness, sorrow, grief

Rad: 忄   Str: 12

悲观	**bēiguān**	pessimistic [5]
悲哀	**bēi'āi**	sad, sorrowful, grieved [6]
悲惨	**bēicǎn**	miserable [6]

Additional words
悲剧 **bēijù** (tragedy).

bèi
carry on one's back, to be burdened, learn by heart, the back of the body

Rad: 月   Str: 9

背	**bèi**	to carry on one's back, to learn by heart, recite from memory [5]
背景	**bèijǐng**	background, backdrop [5]
后背	**hòubèi**	back [5]
背叛	**bèipàn**	to betray [6]
背诵	**bèisòng**	to recite, repeat from memory [6]
违背	**wéibèi**	to violate, run counter to [6]

辈

bèi
lifetime, generation

Rad: 车   Str: 12

一辈子	**yíbèizi**	lifetime, for a lifetime [5]
长辈	**zhǎngbèi**	elder generation [5]

Additional words
先辈 **xiānbèi** (older generation, ancestors).

贝

bèi
cowries, shell, valuables, shellfish

Rad: 贝   Str: 4

宝贝	**bǎobèi**	precious thing, treasured object, darling [5]
贝壳	**bèiké**	shell, conch [6]

彼

bǐ
one another, that, those

Rad: 彳   Str: 8

彼此	**bǐcǐ**	each other, one another [5]

避

bì
avoid, shun, flee, escape, leave

Rad: 辶   Str: 16

避免	**bìmiǎn**	avoid, avert [5]
逃避	**táobì**	evade, shirk [5]
回避	**huíbì**	to evade, to shun, to avoid [6]

bì

to close, stop up, shut, obstruct

Rad: 门   Str: 6

关闭	**guānbì**	to close, shut [5]
闭塞	**bìsè**	stop up, unenlightened, hard to get to [6]
倒闭	**dǎobì**	to go bankrupt, close down [6]
封闭	**fēngbì**	to seal, close, confine, seal off, confined, closed [6]

bì

wall, rampart

Rad: 土   Str: 16

隔壁	**gébì**	next door [5]
悬崖峭壁	**xuányáqiàobì**	cliff [6]

Additional words
墙壁 **qiángbì** (wall); 壁虎 **bìhǔ** (gecko)
壁球 **bìqiú** (squash (game)).

bì

money, coins, currency

Rad: 巾   Str: 4

人民币	**rénmínbì**	Renminbi (RMB), Chinese Yuan (CNY), the name of China's currency [5]
货币	**huòbì**	money, currency [6]

Additional words
硬币 **yìngbì** (coin).

biān

weave, plait, organize, group, arrange, edit, compile, write, compose, fabricate

Rad: 纟   Str: 12

编辑	**biānjí**	edit, compile, editor, compiler [5]
编织	**biānzhī**	knit, weave [6]

biān

a whip, alash, to flog, to slash, to whip

Rad: 革   Str: 18

鞭炮	**biānpào**	firecrackers [5]
鞭策	**biāncè**	to urge on, encourage sb (to make progress) [6]

biàn

dispute, debate, argue, discuss

Rad: 辛   Str: 16

辩论	**biànlùn**	argue, debate, argument [5]
辩护	**biànhù**	to plead, speak in defence of [6]
辩解	**biànjiě**	to explain, to justify, to defend (a point of view etc), to provide an explanation, to try to defend oneself [6]
辩证	**biànzhèng**	dialectical [6]
答辩	**dábiàn**	to reply (to an accusation) [6]

bīng

soldiers, a force, an army, weapons, arms, military, warlike

Rad: 八   Str: 7

士兵	**shìbīng**	soldier, private, enlisted man [5]

Additional words

兵力 **bīnglì** (military strength);
兵役 **bīngyì** (military service);
宪兵 **xiànbīng** (military police).

bō

glass

Rad: 王   Str: 9

玻璃	**bōli**	glass [5]

脖

bó
neck

Rad: 月   Str: 11

脖子	**bózi**	neck [5]

补

bǔ
to repair, to patch, to mend, to make up for, to fill (a vacancy), to supplement

Rad: 衤   Str: 7

补充	**bǔchōng**	replenish, supplement, complement [5]
补偿	**bǔcháng**	compensate, make up for [6]
补救	**bǔjiù**	repair, remedy [6]
补贴	**bǔtiē**	to subsidise, subsidy, allowance [6]
弥补	**míbǔ**	complement, make up for (a deficiency) [6]

布

bù
diffuse, extend, notify, to declare, to announce, cotton cloth

Rad: 巾   Str: 5

布	**bù**	cloth, to declare, to announce, to spread, to make known [5]
分布	**fēnbù**	be distributed, be scattered, be dispersed [5]
公布	**gōngbù**	make public, promulgate, announce, publicise [5]
宣布	**xuānbù**	to declare, announce [5]
颁布	**bānbù**	to issue, to proclaim, to enact (laws, decrees etc) [6]
遍布	**biànbù**	found everywhere, ubiquitous, spread all over [6]
布告	**bùgào**	posting on a bulletin board, notice, bulletin, to announce [6]
布局	**bùjú**	distribution, layout [6]
布置	**bùzhì**	to fix up, arrange, decorate [6]
发布	**fābù**	to issue, put out, announce [6]
瀑布	**pùbù**	waterfall [6]
散布	**sànbù**	scatter, disseminate, spread, sow [6]

cái
money, wealth, riches, property, valuables

Rad: 贝   Str: 7

财产	**cáichǎn**	property, possessions [5]
财富	**cáifù**	riches, wealth [6]
财务	**cáiwù**	financial affairs [6]
财政	**cáizhèng**	government finance, public economy [6]
发财	**fācái**	to get rich [6]

cái
cut, trim, reduce, diminish, decision, judgement

Rad: 衣   Str: 12

总裁	**zǒngcái**	chairman, president [5]
裁缝	**cáifeng**	tailor, dressmaker [6]
裁判	**cáipàn**	judge, umpire, act as referee, referee [6]
裁员	**cáiyuán**	to cut staff, layoff, downsize [6]
独裁	**dúcái**	dictatorship, autocracy [6]
体裁	**tǐcái**	types of literature [6]
制裁	**zhìcái**	to punish, punishment, sanctions (incl. economic) [6]

cǎi
to pick, to pluck, to collect, to select, to choose, to gather, affairs

Rad: 采   Str: 8

采访	**cǎifǎng**	gather news, interview [5]
采取	**cǎiqǔ**	to adopt or carry out (measures, policies, course of action), to take [5]
采购	**cǎigòu**	to purchase [6]
采集	**cǎijí**	to gather, to collect, to harvest [6]
采纳	**cǎinà**	to accept [6]
开采	**kāicǎi**	to extract (ore or other resource from a mine), to exploit, to mine [6]
无精打采	**wújīng dǎcǎi**	listless, dispirited [6]
兴高采烈	**xìnggāo cǎiliè**	be in high spirits, be enraptured [6]

cǎi
step upon, tread on, stamp

Rad: 足   Str: 15

踩   **cǎi**   tread, stamp on [5]

cán
ashamed

Rad: 忄   Str: 11

惭愧   **cánkuì**   ashamed [5]

cáng
to hide away, to conceal, to harbor, store, accumulate, storehouse, depository

Rad: 艹   Str: 17

躲藏	**duǒcáng**	take cover, hide out, dodge [5]
收藏	**shōucáng**	to hoard, to collect, collection [6]
蕴藏	**yùncáng**	to hold in store, contain (untapped reserves etc.) [6]

Additional words
捉迷藏 **zhuō mícáng** (play hide-and-seek).

cāo
to hold, to drill, to exercise, to act, to do, to take in hand, to keep, to manage

Rad: 扌   Str: 16

操场	**cāochǎng**	playground, sports ground [5]
操心	**cāoxīn**	to bother, worry about, take pains [5]
操劳	**cāoláo**	work hard [6]
操练	**cāoliàn**	drill, practice [6]
操纵	**cāozòng**	handle, control, operate, manipulate, rig [6]
操作	**cāozuò**	operate, manipulate [6]

糙 cāo
rough, coarse (in texture)

Rad: 米   Str: 16

粗糙	**cūcāo**	crude, rough [5]

册 cè
book, booklet, measure word (for books)

Rad: 丿   Str: 5

册	**cè**	book, booklet, measure word (for books) [5]
注册	**zhùcè**	enrol, register [5]

Additional words
手册 **shǒucè** (handbook).

测 cè
side, to lean, to survey, to measure, conjecture

Rad: 氵   Str: 9

测验	**cèyàn**	test, examination [5]
测量	**cèliáng**	survey, to measure, to gauge, to determine [6]
探测	**tàncè**	to explore, probe [6]
推测	**tuīcè**	speculate, guess, presume [6]

Additional words
观测 **guāncè** (observe).

曾 céng
already, at some time in the past, before, once

Rad: 曰   Str: 12

曾经	**céngjīng**	once, already, former, previously, ever, past tense marker (used before verb or clause) [5]

chā

fork, pitchfork, prong, pick, cross, intersect

Rad: 又   Str: 3

叉子	**chāzi**	fork [5]
交叉	**jiāochā**	to intersect, cross [6]

chā

insert, stick in, pierce, to take part in, to interfere, to interpose

Rad: 扌   Str: 12

插	**chā**	to insert, stick in, interfere [5]
插座	**chāzuò**	socket, power outlet [6]

Additional words
插头 **chātóu** (plug).

chāi

to tear open, to tear down, to tear apart, to open

Rad: 扌   Str: 8

拆	**chāi**	to tear down, knock down [5]

chái

firewood

Rad: 木   Str: 10

火柴	**huǒchái**	match (for lighting fire) [5]
柴油	**cháiyóu**	diesel oil [6]

Additional words
砍柴 **kǎnchái** (cut firewood).

chǎn
to give birth to, produce, product, resources, estate

Rad: 亠   Str: 6

财产	**cáichǎn**	property, possessions [5]
产品	**chǎnpǐn**	goods, merchandise, product [5]
产生	**chǎnshēng**	produce, take place, engender [5]
破产	**pòchǎn**	to go bankrupt, go broke [5]
生产	**shēngchǎn**	childbirth, to produce, manufacture, production [5]
产业	**chǎnyè**	industry, estate, property, industrial [6]
矿产	**kuàngchǎn**	minerals, mineral products [6]
盛产	**shèngchǎn**	abound in, teem with [6]
遗产	**yíchǎn**	heritage, legacy, inheritance [6]
资产	**zīchǎn**	capital, asset [6]

Additional words
共产党 **Gòngchǎndǎng** (Communist Party).

cháng
to compensate, pay back, to recompense

Rad: 亻   Str: 11

赔偿	**péicháng**	to compensate [5]
补偿	**bǔcháng**	compensate, make up for [6]
偿还	**chánghuán**	to repay, compensate [6]
得不偿失	**débù chángshī**	the gains do not make up for the losses [6]
无偿	**wúcháng**	free, no charge, at no cost [6]

cháng
intestines

Rad: 月   Str: 7

| 香肠 | **xiāngcháng** | sausage [5] |

Additional words
腊肠 **làcháng** (sausage).

chǎng

cliff, slope, factory, yard, depot, workhouse, works, (industrial) plant

Rad: 厂　Str: 2

| 工厂 | **gōngchǎng** | factory [5] |

chàng

initiate, instigate, introduce, lead

Rad: 亻　Str: 10

提倡	**tíchàng**	to advocate, promote [5]
倡导	**chàngdǎo**	to advocate, be a proponent of [6]
倡议	**chàngyì**	to suggest, to initiate, proposal, initiative [6]

chāo

to copy, to plagiarize, to search and seize, to go, to transcribe, to take a shortcut

Rad: 扌　Str: 7

| 抄 | **chāo** | to copy, plagiarise [5] |

Additional words
抄写 **chāoxiě** (transcribe).

cháo

to face, towards, facing, direct, a dynasty, the imperial court, (abbr.) Korea, esp. N. Korea

zhāo

morning

Rad: 月　Str: 12

朝	**cháo**	towards, facing, imperial or royal court, dynasty [5]
朝代	**cháodài**	dynasty [6]
朝气蓬勃	**zhāoqì** **péngbó**	full of youthful spirit, vigour [6]

Additional words
朝鲜 **Cháoxiān** (Korea).

cháo
tide, current, damp, moist, humid

Rad: 氵 Str: 15

潮湿	**cháoshī**	wet, humid, damp, moist [5]
潮流	**cháoliú**	tide, tidal current, trend [6]
高潮	**gāocháo**	high tide, upsurge, climax, orgasm [6]

chǎo
to quarrel, to make a noise, noisy, to disturb by making a noise

Rad: 口 Str: 7

吵	**chǎo**	to quarrel, make a noise, noisy [5]
吵架	**chǎojià**	to quarrel, argue [5]

chǎo
saute, pan-fry, to fry, fried

Rad: 火 Str: 8

炒	**chǎo**	stir fry, saute [5]

Additional words
炒饭 **chǎofàn** (fried rice).

chè
pervade, penetrate, pass through, thorough, penetrating

Rad: 彳 Str: 7

彻底	**chèdǐ**	thoroughgoing, thorough [5]
贯彻	**guànchè**	carry out, implement [6]

chén

submerge, immerse, sink, deep, profound, to lower, to drop

Rad: 氵 Str: 7

chēng

balanced, to fit, well-off, suitable, to call, to praise, to weigh, to estimate, to consider, to call, to address, to name, to say, commend

chèn

symmetric

Rad: 禾 Str: 10

沉默	chénmò	silent, uncommunicative [5]
沉淀	chéndiàn	to settle, precipitate (solid sediment out of a solution) [6]
沉闷	chénmèn	oppressive, withdrawn [6]
沉思	chénsī	to muse, ponder, meditate, contemplate [6]
沉重	chénzhòng	heavy, hard, serious, critical [6]
沉着	chénzhuó	composed, cool headed [6]
深沉	shēnchén	deep, extreme, dull, low pitched (sound) [6]

称	chēng	to weigh, state, name [5]
称呼	chēnghu	call, address, name, term of address [5]
称赞	chēngzàn	praise, acclaim, commend [5]
称心如意	chènxīn rúyì	everything one could wish for [6]
称号	chēnghào	title, term of address [6]
对称	duìchèn	symmetrical, symmetry [6]

chèn

avail oneself of, take advantage of

Rad: 走 Str: 12

chén

dust, dirt, earth

Rad: 小 Str: 6

趁	chèn	avail oneself of [5]

灰尘	huīchén	dust [5]

chéng

to bear, to carry, to hold, to continue, to undertake, to take charge, owing to, due to, to receive

Rad: 手   Str: 8

承担	chéngdān	to undertake, assume (responsibility etc.) [5]
承认	chéngrèn	to admit, recognise, acknowledge [5]
承受	chéngshòu	to bear, to support, to inherit [5]
承办	chéngbàn	to undertake, to accept a contract [6]
承包	chéngbāo	contract (with), assume full responsibility [6]
承诺	chéngnuò	promise, commitment [6]
继承	jìchéng	inherit, succeed, carry on, carry forward [6]

chí

pond, reservoir

Rad: 氵   Str: 6

| 池塘 | chítáng | pool, pond [5] |
| 电池 | diànchí | battery, electric cell [5] |

Additional words
游泳池 **yóuyǒngchí** (swimming pool).

chǐ

a Chinese foot (one-third of a metre), a ruler, a note musical note on traditional Chinese scale

Rad: 尸   Str: 4

| 尺子 | chǐzi | ruler, rule [5] |

Additional words
英尺 **yīngchǐ** (foot (unit of measurement)).

chǐ

tooth

Rad: 齿   Str: 8

| 牙齿 | yáchǐ | tooth [5] |

chì
wing

Rad: 羽   Str: 10

翅膀   **chìbǎng**   wing [5]

chóng
insect, worm, an invertebrate

Rad: 虫   Str: 6

昆虫   **kūnchóng**   insect [5]

<u>Additional words</u>
害虫 **hàichóng** (destructive insect);
寄生虫 **jìshēngchóng** (parasite);
爬虫 **páchóng** (reptile).

chōng
fill, satisfy, fulfill, to act in place of, substitute, sufficient, full

Rad: 亠   Str: 6

补充	**bǔchōng**	replenish, supplement, complement [5]
充电器	**chōngdiànqì**	electric charger [5]
充分	**chōngfèn**	ample, full, abundant [5]
充满	**chōngmǎn**	brimming with, full of [5]
充当	**chōngdāng**	act as, serve as [6]
充沛	**chōngpèi**	abundant, plentiful [6]
充实	**chōngshí**	substantial, rich, to substantiate, enrich, fill [6]
充足	**chōngzú**	adequate, abundant [6]
扩充	**kuòchōng**	extend, enlarge [6]
冒充	**màochōng**	imitate, imitation [6]

chōng
to rinse, to collide, to water, to rush, to dash (against), to wash out, to charge, forceful, dynamic, to punch

Rad: 氵   Str: 6

冲	**chōng**	to rinse, to collide with, to dash against, to mix with water, to develop (a film), to flush (a toilet) [5]
冲动	**chōngdòng**	impulse, impulsive [6]
冲击	**chōngjī**	impact, shock, pound, attack [6]
冲突	**chōngtū**	collide, conflict, clash, collision [6]

<u>Additional words</u>
冲锋 **chōngfēng** (charge, assault);
俯冲 **fǔchōng** (dive).

chǒng

to love, to pamper, to spoil, to favor

Rad: 宀   Str: 8

宠物   **chǒngwù**   pet (in the home) [5]

chóu

silk

Rad: 纟   Str: 11

丝绸   **sīchóu**   silk [5]

chóu

worry about

Rad: 心   Str: 13

发愁   **fāchóu**   worry, be anxious [5]

chǒu

clown, shameful, ugly, disgraceful, 2nd Earthly Branch

Rad: 一   Str: 4

| 丑 | **chǒu** | ugly, unsightly, bad-looking, detestable, shameful, clown, 1-3 a.m. [5] |
| 丑恶 | **chǒu'è** | ugly, repulsive [6] |

Additional words
丑陋 **chǒulòu** (ugly, disgraceful, scandalous).

chòu

stench, stink, smelly, to smell (bad)

Rad: 自   Str: 10

臭	**chòu**	smelly, to smell (bad) [5]

chū

at first, (at the) beginning, first, junior, basic

Rad: 刀   Str: 7

初级	**chūjí**	elementary, primary [5]
最初	**zuìchū**	first, initial [5]
初步	**chūbù**	initial, preliminary [6]
当初	**dāngchū**	in the beginning, at that time, originally [6]
起初	**qǐchū**	at first, in the beginning, originally [6]

chù

knock against, touch, to feel

Rad: 角   Str: 13

接触	**jiēchù**	to contact, get in touch [5]
触犯	**chùfàn**	to offend, violate [6]

chuǎng

to rush, break through

Rad: 门   Str: 6

闯	**chuǎng**	to rush, charge, dash [5]

chuàng
a wound, cut, injury, begin, initiate, inaugurate, start, create

Rad: 刂   Str: 6

<u>Notes</u>
Also pronounced **chuāng** (trauma).

创造	**chuàngzào**	to create, to bring about, to produce [5]
创立	**chuànglì**	found, establish, initiate [6]
创新	**chuàngxīn**	innovate, innovation, creativity, fresh idea [6]
创业	**chuàngyè**	to begin an undertaking, to start a major task, to initiate, to venture, venture [6]
创作	**chuàngzuò**	create, write, creative work [6]

<u>Additional words</u>
创伤 **chuāngshāng** (trauma).

chuī
to blow, blast, puff, boast, brag, end in failure

Rad: 口   Str: 7

吹	**chuī**	to blow, to play (a wind instrument), brag, boast, end in failure [5]
吹牛	**chuīniú**	brag, boast [6]
吹捧	**chuīpěng**	flatter, adulation [6]

chún
pure, simple, unmixed, genuine

Rad: 纟   Str: 7

单纯	**dānchún**	simple, pure, uncomplicated [5]
纯粹	**chúncuì**	pure, purely, purity [6]
纯洁	**chúnjié**	pure, unadulterated, purify, cleanse [6]

cí
bid farewell, resign, say goodbye, take leave, decline

Rad: 辛   Str: 13

辞职	**cízhí**	to resign [5]
推辞	**tuīcí**	to decline, refuse, turn down (an offer) [5]
告辞	**gàocí**	to say goodbye, bid farewell, take leave [6]
致辞	**zhìcí**	oration, to address (an audience) [6]

刺

cì
thorn, sting, prick, pierce, stab

Rad: 刂   Str: 8

刺激	**cìjī**	stimulate, irritate, provoke, stimulus, provocation [5]
讽刺	**fěngcì**	satirise, ridicule, mock [5]
刺	**cì**	thorn, sting, prick, pierce, stab, thrust [6]

匆

cōng
hurried, hasty

Rad: 勹   Str: 5

匆忙	**cōngmáng**	hurried, hasty [5]

Additional words
匆匆 **cōngcōng** (hurriedly, obviously, apparently).

促

cù
to hurry, to rush, to hasten, near, to promote

Rad: 亻   Str: 9

促进	**cùjìn**	to promote (an idea or cause), to advance, boost [5]
促使	**cùshǐ**	to urge, impel, push, spur on [5]
仓促	**cāngcù**	hurried [6]
督促	**dūcù**	to urge sb to complete a task [6]
短促	**duǎncù**	very brief [6]

醋

cù
vinegar

Rad: 酉   Str: 15

醋	**cù**	vinegar [5]

Additional words
吃醋 **chīcù** (be jealous (e.g. in love affair));
糖醋 **tángcù** (sweet and sour).

催 cuī
urge, press, expedite, prompt, hurry

Rad: 亻　Str: 13

| 催 | cuī | press, urge [5] |

脆 cuì
crisp, brittle, clear and loud voice

Rad: 月　Str: 10

| 干脆 | gāncuì | straightforward, clear-cut, simple, just [5] |
| 脆弱 | cuìruò | flimsy, frail [6] |

村 cūn
village

Rad: 木　Str: 7

| 农村 | nóngcūn | rural area, countryside, village [5] |

措 cuò
put in order, arrange, administer, execute, take action on

Rad: 扌　Str: 11

| 措施 | cuòshī | measure, step (to be taken) [5] |

dá
reach, attain, pass through, realize, inform, dignity

Rad: 辶   Str: 6

表达	**biǎodá**	to express, convey, voice an opinion [5]
达到	**dádào**	achieve, attain, reach [5]
到达	**dàodá**	arrive, reach, get to [5]
发达	**fādá**	developed, flourishing [5]
传达	**chuándá**	to convey, transmit, communicate [6]
达成	**dáchéng**	reach (agreement), conclude (negotiation) [6]
抵达	**dǐdá**	arrive, reach (a destination) [6]
雷达	**léidá**	radar (loan word) [6]
转达	**zhuǎndá**	to pass on, convey, communicate [6]

dāi
foolish, stupid, no expression, stay, stay, stupid

Rad: 口   Str: 7

| 呆 | **dāi** | foolish, stupid, no expression, to stay [5] |
| 发呆 | **fādāi** | lost in thought, to stare blankly [6] |

Additional words
呆板 **dāibǎn** (stiff).

dài
represent, generation, period, epoch, age, era

Rad: 亻   Str: 5

代表	**dàibiǎo**	to represent, on behalf of, representative [5]
代替	**dàitì**	instead, to replace, to substitute [5]
古代	**gǔdài**	ancient times, olden times [5]
近代	**jìndài**	modern times [5]
年代	**niándài**	a decade of a century (e.g. the Sixties), age, era, period [5]
时代	**shídài**	times, age, era, epoch [5]
现代	**xiàndài**	modern times, the contemporary age [5]
朝代	**cháodài**	dynasty [6]
代价	**dàijià**	cost, price, expense [6]
代理	**dàilǐ**	to act as an agent, deputise [6]
当代	**dāngdài**	present time, contemporary age, nowadays [6]
后代	**hòudài**	offspring, descendant, posterity, later generation [6]
交代	**jiāodài**	to hand over, explain, make clear, account for, justify oneself [6]
历代	**lìdài**	successive generations, successive dynasties, past dynasties [6]
世代	**shìdài**	generation, an era, accumulation of years, passing on from generation to generation [6]
新陈代谢	**xīnchén dàixiè**	metabolism [6]

贷 dài

lend on interest, borrow, loan, make excuses, pardon, forgive

Rad: 贝   Str: 9

| 贷款 | **dàikuǎn** | a loan, to provide a loan (e.g. a bank) [5] |

耽 dān

indulge, delay

Rad: 耳   Str: 10

| 耽误 | **dānwu** | delay, waste time [5] |

待 dài

stay, delay, wait, treat, deal with, need, about, intending to do something

Rad: 彳   Str: 9

待遇	**dàiyù**	treatment, compensation, pay, wage, salary [5]
等待	**děngdài**	to wait for, await [5]
对待	**duìdài**	treat, approach [5]
接待	**jiēdài**	to receive (a visitor), to admit (allow sb to enter) [5]
期待	**qīdài**	to expect, look forward to [5]
招待	**zhāodài**	receive, entertain (guests) [5]
看待	**kàndài**	to look upon, to regard [6]
款待	**kuǎndài**	entertain cordially, treat cordially [6]
亏待	**kuīdài**	treat unfairly [6]
虐待	**nüèdài**	to abuse, mistreat [6]
迫不及待	**pòbùjídài**	can't wait (for), be really excited about [6]

Additional words
守株待兔 **shǒuzhūdàitù** (trust to chance and luck in one's actions, hope for gains without pains (lit. guarding a tree trunk to wait for a rabbit)).

dǎn
gall, nerve, courage, guts, gall bladder

Rad: 月　　Str: 9

| 胆小鬼 | **dǎnxiǎoguǐ** | coward [5] |
| 胆怯 | **dǎnqiè** | timid, cowardly [6] |

dàn
insipid, diluted, weak, light in color, tasteless, fresh, indifferent, nitrogen

Rad: 氵　　Str: 11

淡	**dàn**	thin, weak, diluted [5]
冷淡	**lěngdàn**	indifference, unconcerned [5]
清淡	**qīngdàn**	light (of food, not greasy or strongly flavoured), insipid [5]
淡季	**dànjì**	low season [6]
淡水	**dànshuǐ**	fresh water [6]

Additional words
淡蓝 **dànlán** (light blue).

dàn
dawn, morning, day-break, day

Rad: 日　　Str: 5

| 一旦 | **yídàn** | once, in case, in one day [5] |
| 元旦 | **yuándàn** | New Year's Day [5] |

dǎng
hinder, resist, obstruct, hinder, cover, keep off, a cover, to block, to get in the way of, arrange, put in order

Rad: 扌　　Str: 9

| 挡 | **dǎng** | to resist, obstruct, block [5] |
| 遮挡 | **zhēdǎng** | keep out, shelter from [6] |

dàng

cross-piece, official records, grade (of goods), file, records, shelves

Rad: 木   Str: 10

高档	**gāodàng**	superior quality, high grade [5]
搭档	**dādàng**	to cooperate, partner [6]
档案	**dàng'àn**	files, archives, records, dossiers [6]
档次	**dàngcì**	grade, class, quality, level [6]

dǎo

island

Rad: 山   Str: 7

| 岛屿 | **dǎoyǔ** | islands and islets [5] |

dé

virtue, goodness, morality, ethics, kindness, favor, character, kind, Germany

Rad: 彳   Str: 15

| 道德 | **dàodé** | morals, ethics [5] |
| 品德 | **pǐndé** | moral character [6] |

Additional words
穆罕默德 **Mǔhǎnmòdé** (Mohammed);
德国 **déguó** (Germany).

dī

a drop, to drip

Rad: 氵   Str: 14

| 滴 | **dī** | a drop, to drip [5] |

敌 dí
enemy, match

Rad: 攵　Str: 10

敌人	**dírén**	enemy, foe [5]
敌视	**díshì**	be hostile to, antagonise [6]

Additional words
敌军 **díjūn** (enemy troops).

递 dì
to hand over, to pass, to give

Rad: 辶　Str: 10

递	**dì**	to pass on, to hand over [5]
递增	**dìzēng**	increase by degrees [6]

Additional words
递交 **dìjiāo** (deliver, hand on, present, submit).

钓 diào
to fish with a hook and bait

Rad: 钅　Str: 8

钓	**diào**	to fish (with a hook and bait) [5]

Additional words
钓钩 **diàogōu** (fishing hook).

蝶 dié
butterfly

Rad: 虫　Str: 15

蝴蝶	**húdié**	butterfly [5]

Additional words
蝶蛹 **diéyǒng** (chrysalis).

dǐng

peak, top, most, go against, to replace, to substitute, measure word (for hats, headwear, veils)

Rad: 页   Str: 8

顶   **dǐng**   peak, top, most, go against, to substitute, measure word (for hats, headwear, veils) [5]

Additional words
屋顶 **wūdǐng** (roof); 一顶帽子 **yì dǐng màozi** (a hat).

dìng

to agree, to conclude, to draw up, to subscribe to (a newspaper, etc.), to order

Rad: 讠   Str: 4

预订   **yùdìng**   to book ahead, place an order [5]

dòng

to freeze

Rad: 冫   Str: 7

| 冻 | **dòng** | freeze [5] |
| 冻结 | **dòngjié** | to freeze (loan, wage, price etc) [6] |

dòng

cave, hole

Rad: 氵   Str: 9

| 洞 | **dòng** | hole, cave [5] |
| 空洞 | **kōngdòng** | empty, hollow, shallow, vacuous, cavity [6] |

Additional words
窑洞 **yáodòng** (cave dwelling).

dǒu
to fight, to battle, to struggle, to incite, fight, incite

dòu
fight

Rad: 斗   Str: 4

dǒu
tremble

Rad: 扌   Str: 7

奋斗	**fèndòu**	to fight, struggle, strive [5]
搏斗	**bódòu**	to struggle, fight [6]
斗争	**dòuzhēng**	fight, struggle, combat [6]
泰斗	**tàidǒu**	leading authority, scholar [6]
战斗	**zhàndòu**	to fight, to battle [6]

发抖	**fādǒu**	tremble [5]
颤抖	**chàndǒu**	tremble, shiver, shake [6]

Additional words
烟斗 **yāndǒu** (tobacco or opium pipe).

dòu
bean, peas

Rad: 豆   Str: 7

dòu
linger

Rad: 辶   Str: 10

豆腐	**dòufu**	tofu, bean curd [5]
土豆	**tǔdòu**	potato [5]

逗	**dòu**	tease, provoke [5]

dú

alone, independent, single, sole, only

Rad: 犭　Str: 9

单独	**dāndú**	alone, lone, solitary [5]
独立	**dúlì**	stand alone, independence [5]
独特	**dútè**	unique, distinctive, original [5]
得天独厚	**détiān dúhòu**	rich in resources (of an area of land), gifted (of a person) [6]
独裁	**dúcái**	dictatorship, autocracy [6]
孤独	**gūdú**	lonely [6]
唯独	**wéidú**	alone, only, unique [6]

dú

poison, narcotics

Rad: 母　Str: 9

病毒	**bìngdú**	virus [5]
毒品	**dúpǐn**	drugs, narcotics, poison [6]
消毒	**xiāodú**	to disinfect, sterilise, sanitise [6]

Additional words
毒物 **dúwù** (poison).

duī

a pile, a mass, heap, stack

Rad: 土　Str: 11

| 堆 | **duī** | a pile, a mass, heap, stack [5] |
| 堆积 | **duījī** | pile up, heap up, accumulate [6] |

duì

to cash

Rad: ㆍˊ　Str: 7

| 兑换 | **duìhuàn** | to exchange, convert (currencies) [5] |
| 兑现 | **duìxiàn** | to cash (a cheque etc.), honour a commitment [6] |

dūn
ton

Rad: 口   Str: 7

| 吨 | **dūn** | ton [5] |

踌

dūn
crouch, squat

Rad: 足   Str: 19

| 蹲 | **dūn** | crouch, squat [5] |

dùn
a time, jerk, stop, meal, bout, spell, measure word (for meals, beatings, tellings off etc.)

Rad: 页   Str: 10

顿	**dùn**	stop, pause, measure word (for meals, beatings, tellings off etc.) [5]
顿时	**dùnshí**	immediately, at once, suddenly [6]
停顿	**tíngdùn**	pause, halt [6]
整顿	**zhěngdùn**	to restructure, consolidate, reorganise [6]

盾

dùn
shield

Rad: 目   Str: 9

| 矛盾 | **máodùn** | contradiction, contradictory (lit. spear-shield) [5] |

躲 duǒ

avoid, get out of way, to hide, to go into hiding

Rad: 身   Str: 13

| 躲藏 | **duǒcáng** | take cover, hide out, dodge [5] |

恶 è

nauseated, evil, to hate, to loathe

wù

hate

ě

nauseous

Rad: 心   Str: 10

恶劣	**èliè**	vile, nasty, disgusting [5]
丑恶	**chǒu'è**	ugly, repulsive [6]
恶心	**ěxin**	feel like vomiting, feel sick, be disgusted [6]
恶化	**èhuà**	worsen, deteriorate, exacerbate [6]
可恶	**kěwù**	loathsome, hateful [6]
凶恶	**xiōng'è**	fierce, ferocious, fiendish, vicious [6]
厌恶	**yànwù**	to loathe, hate, detest [6]

罚 fá

to punish, to penalize

Rad: 罒   Str: 9

罚款	**fákuǎn**	penalty, fine (monetary), to impose a fine [5]
惩罚	**chéngfá**	to punish, punishment, penalty [6]

乏 fá

short of, tired

Rad: 丿   Str: 4

缺乏	**quēfá**	be short of, lack [5]
贫乏	**pínfá**	lack, lacking, incomplete [6]

Additional words
疲乏 **pífá** (tired).

fán

complicated, many, in great numbers

Rad: 糸   Str: 17

繁荣	**fánróng**	flourishing, prosperous, prosperity [5]
繁华	**fánhuá**	flourishing, bustling [6]
繁忙	**fánmáng**	busy, bustling [6]
繁体字	**fántǐzì**	traditional Chinese character [6]
繁殖	**fánzhí**	propagate, breed, reproduce [6]
频繁	**pínfán**	often, frequently [6]

fǎn

to return (to)

Rad: 辶   Str: 7

| 往返 | **wǎngfǎn** | to and from, out and home [5] |

fàn

pattern, model, example

Rad: 艹   Str: 8

范围	**fànwéi**	scope, limits, range [5]
范畴	**fànchóu**	category [6]
规范	**guīfàn**	norm, standard [6]
模范	**mófàn**	model, fine example [6]
师范	**shīfàn**	teacher training, pedagogical, normal (school, e.g. Beijing Normal University) [6]
示范	**shìfàn**	to lead the way, demonstrate, model example [6]

fàn

broad, vast, float, pan-, general, vague

Rad: 氵   Str: 7

| 广泛 | **guǎngfàn** | extensive, wide, ranging, widespread [5] |
| 泛滥 | **fànlàn** | flood, overflow, spread unchecked [6] |

fáng
hinder, harm

Rad: 女   Str: 7

| 妨碍 | **fáng'ài** | hinder, hamper, obstruct, impede, make difficult [5] |
| 不妨 | **bùfáng** | might as well, no harm in [6] |

fáng
to protect, to defend, to guard (against)

Rad: 阝   Str: 6

预防	**yùfáng**	prevent, take precautions against [5]
防守	**fángshǒu**	defend, guard (against) [6]
防御	**fángyù**	defend and resist, guard, defence [6]
防止	**fángzhǐ**	to prevent, avoid, guard against [6]
防治	**fángzhì**	prevent and treat (diseases) [6]
国防	**guófáng**	national defence [6]
消防	**xiāofáng**	fire control, fire fighting [6]

fǎng
to imitate, to copy, seemingly

Rad: 亻   Str: 6

| 仿佛 | **fǎngfú** | to seem, as if [5] |
| 模仿 | **mófǎng** | copy, imitate [5] |

fǎng
inquire, seek, visit

Rad: 讠   Str: 6

采访	**cǎifǎng**	gather news, interview [5]
拜访	**bàifǎng**	pay a visit, call on [6]
访问	**fǎngwèn**	to visit, call on [6]

fèi
abolish, crippled

Rad: 广   Str: 8

废话	**fèihuà**	nonsense, superfluous words, rubbish [5]
半途而废	**bàntú érfèi**	give up halfway, leave sth unfinished [6]
废除	**fèichú**	abolish, annul, abrogate, repeal [6]
废寝忘食	**fèiqǐn wàngshí**	be so absorbed as to forget to eat and sleep [6]
废墟	**fèixū**	ruins, remains of a place destroyed [6]
作废	**zuòfèi**	to cancel, cancellation [6]

fēn
numerous, confused, disorderly

Rad: 纟   Str: 7

| 纷纷 | **fēnfēn** | one after another [5] |
| 纠纷 | **jiūfēn** | dispute, entanglement (law) [6] |

fēn
miasma, vapor

Rad: 气   Str: 8

| 气氛 | **qìfēn** | atmosphere, ambience [5] |

fēng
insane, mad, wild

Rad: 广   Str: 9

| 疯狂 | **fēngkuáng** | crazy, maniac, mad, wild, frenzied, unbridled [5] |

蜂 **fēng**
bee, wasp

Rad: 虫   Str: 13

蜜蜂   **mìfēng**   bee, honeybee [5]

Additional words
马蜂 **mǎfēng** (hornet, wasp).

讽 **fěng**
satirize

Rad: 讠   Str: 6

讽刺   **fěngcì**   satirise, ridicule, mock [5]

Additional words
嘲讽 **cháofěng** (sneer at, taunt, mock);
讥讽 **jīfěng** (ridicule).

佛 **fú**
seem

Rad: 亻   Str: 7

Notes
Also pronounced **fó** (Buddha, Buddhism).

仿佛   **fǎngfú**   to seem, as if [5]

Additional words
佛教 **Fójiào** (Buddhism).

扶 **fú**
to support with hand, to help sb. up, to help

Rad: 扌   Str: 7

扶   **fú**   support with the hand, help sb up [5]

fú
width, roll, measure word (for pictures, paintings, textile)

Rad: 巾　Str: 12

幅	**fú**	width, roll, measure word (for pictures, paintings etc.) [5]
幅度	**fúdù**	width, extent, range, scope [6]

Additional words
一幅画 **yīfúhuà** (a picture).

fǔ
to assist, to complement, auxiliary

Rad: 车　Str: 11

辅导	**fǔdǎo**	to coach, to tutor, to give advice (in study) [5]
辅助	**fǔzhù**	to assist, aid [6]
相辅相成	**xiāngfǔ xiāngchéng**	to complement one another [6]

腐

fǔ
decay, rotten

Rad: 肉　Str: 14

豆腐	**dòufu**	tofu, bean curd [5]
腐败	**fǔbài**	corrupt, corruption [6]
腐烂	**fǔlàn**	rot, perish [6]
腐蚀	**fǔshí**	erode, corrode, corrupt, pervert [6]
腐朽	**fǔxiǔ**	rotten, decayed, mouldering, degenerate, decadent [6]

府

fǔ
prefecture, mansion

Rad: 广　Str: 8

政府	**zhèngfǔ**	government [5]

fù
woman

Rad: 女　　Str: 6

妇女	**fùnǚ**	woman [5]
夫妇	**fūfù**	husband and wife, married couple [6]
媳妇	**xífu**	son's wife, daughter-in-law [6]

Additional words
寡妇 **guǎfu** (widow).

gài
lid, top, cover, canopy, to build

Rad: 皿　　Str: 11

盖	**gài**	cover, lid, top [5]
覆盖	**fùgài**	overlay, cover with [6]
盖章	**gàizhāng**	to affix a seal [6]
膝盖	**xīgài**	knee [6]
掩盖	**yǎngài**	cover up, conceal, hide, cloak [6]

Additional words
盖子 **gàizi** (lid).

gāng
guiding principle, key link, head rope of a fishing net, class (taxonomy), outline, program

Rad: 纟　　Str: 7

提纲	**tígāng**	outline [5]
纲领	**gānglǐng**	guiding principle, program, platform [6]

gǎo
to do, to make, to go in for, to set up, to get hold of, to take care of

Rad: 扌　　Str: 13

搞	**gǎo**	do, cause, make, get hold of [5]

 **gé**
to separate, to stand or lie between, to divide, to cut off

Rad: 阝   Str: 12

隔壁	**gébì**	next door [5]
隔阂	**géhé**	estrangement, misunderstanding, gulf, barrier [6]
隔离	**gélí**	to insulate, separate [6]
间隔	**jiàngé**	interval, gap, space [6]

 **gé**
leather, remove

Rad: 革   Str: 9

改革	**gǎigé**	to reform [5]
革命	**gémìng**	revolution, revolutionary (politics) [6]
皮革	**pígé**	leather [6]

gōng
respectful

Rad: 小   Str: 10

| 恭喜 | **gōngxǐ** | congratulate, congratulations [5] |
| 恭敬 | **gōngjìng** | dutiful, respectful [6] |

Additional words
恭贺新禧 **gōnghèxīnxǐ** (Happy New Year).

 **gòng**
tribute, gifts

Rad: 贝   Str: 7

| 贡献 | **gòngxiàn** | contribute, dedicate, contribution [5] |

gōu
ditch, gutter

Rad: 氵　Str: 7

沟通	**gōutōng**	communicate [5]

gòu
to construct, to form, to make up, to compose

Rad: 木　Str: 8

构成	**gòuchéng**	to compose, constitute [5]
结构	**jiégòu**	structure, composition [5]
构思	**gòusī**	to outline a story, to make a preliminary sketch, conceive, design [6]
机构	**jīgòu**	mechanism, structure, organization, agency, institution [6]

gū
paternal aunt

Rad: 女　Str: 8

姑姑	**gūgu**	father's sister [5]
姑娘	**gūniang**	girl, young woman, daughter [5]
姑且	**gūqiě**	temporarily, the time being, for the moment, provisional, tentatively [6]

gǔ
ancient, old

Rad: 口　Str: 5

古代	**gǔdài**	ancient times, olden times [5]
古典	**gǔdiǎn**	classical [5]
名胜古迹	**míngshèng gǔjì**	place of historical interest [5]
古董	**gǔdǒng**	antique [6]
古怪	**gǔguài**	eccentric, grotesque [6]
考古	**kǎogǔ**	archaeology [6]

股

gǔ
share, portion, section, part, thigh, measure word (for electric current)

Rad: 月   Str: 8

股票	**gǔpiào**	shares, stock [5]
股东	**gǔdōng**	stockholder [6]
股份	**gǔfèn**	share (in a company), stock [6]
屁股	**pìgu**	buttocks, bottom, butt [6]

骨

gǔ
bone

Rad: 骨   Str: 9

骨头	**gǔtou**	bone, strong character [5]
骨干	**gǔgàn**	diaphysis (long segment of a bone), backbone (figurative) [6]

固

gù
hard, strong, solid, sure

Rad: 囗   Str: 8

固定	**gùdìng**	fixed, regular, predetermined, to fix, fasten, regularise [5]
根深蒂固	**gēnshēn dìgù**	deep rooted (problem etc) [6]
巩固	**gǒnggù**	strong, solidify, consolidate, strengthen [6]
固然	**gùrán**	it is true, admittedly, no doubt, indeed, certainly [6]
固体	**gùtǐ**	solid, solid body [6]
固有	**gùyǒu**	intrinsic to sth, inherent [6]
固执	**gùzhi**	stubborn [6]
坚固	**jiāngù**	solid, firm, sturdy, strong, impregnable [6]
牢固	**láogù**	solid, strong, firm, secure [6]
凝固	**nínggù**	to congeal, solidify, with rapt attention (figurative) [6]
顽固	**wángù**	obstinate, stubborn [6]

乖
guāi
obedient, well-behaved, clever

Rad: 丿 Str: 8

| 乖 | **guāi** | obedient, well-behaved (of a child), good, clever, shrewd, lovely [5] |

拐
guǎi
kidnap, to turn

Rad: 扌 Str: 8

| 拐弯 | **guǎiwān** | turn a corner, make a turn, change direction [5] |
| 拐杖 | **guǎizhàng** | crutch, walking stick [6] |

Additional words
拐棍 **guǎigùn** (walking stick).

guān
official, government

Rad: 宀 Str: 8

官	**guān**	official, government [5]
打官司	**dǎguānsi**	to sue, file a lawsuit [6]
官方	**guānfāng**	by the government official [6]
器官	**qìguān**	organ (part of body tissue), apparatus [6]

Additional words
官僚 **guānliáo** (bureaucrat).

冠
guàn
first place

Rad: 冖 Str: 9

| 冠军 | **guànjūn** | champion [5] |

guī
to go back, to return

Rad: 彐   Str: 5

归纳	**guīnà**	conclude [5]
归根到底	**guīgēn dàodǐ**	to sum up, in the final analysis [6]
归还	**guīhuán**	to return sth, to revert [6]

guǐ
ghost, sly, crafty

Rad: 鬼   Str: 9

| 胆小鬼 | **dǎnxiǎoguǐ** | coward [5] |
| 魔鬼 | **móguǐ** | devil, demon [6] |

guì
cupboard, cabinet, wardrobe

Rad: 木   Str: 8

| 柜台 | **guìtái** | counter, bar [5] |

Additional words
衣柜 **yīguì** (wardrobe).

gǔn
to boil, to roll

Rad: 氵   Str: 13

| 滚 | **gǔn** | to boil, roll [5] |
| 摇滚 | **yáogǔn** | rock 'n' roll, rock [6] |

guō
pot, pan, boiler

Rad: 钅 Str: 12

| 锅 | **guō** | pan, pot [5] |
| 涮火锅 | **shuànhuǒguō** | hotpot [6] |

Additional words
锅贴 **guōtiē** (fried dumpling).

guǒ
wrap around

Rad: 衣 Str: 14

| 包裹 | **bāoguǒ** | package, parcel [5] |

hā
laughter, yawn, a
Pekinese, a pug

Rad: 口 Str: 9

| 哈 | **hā** | laughter, yawn [5] |

Additional words
哈欠 **hāqiàn** (yawn).

hán
to keep, to contain

Rad: 口 Str: 7

包含	**bāohán**	contain, embody, include [5]
含糊	**hánhu**	ambiguous, vague, unsure, careless, perfunctory [6]
含义	**hányì**	signification, meaning [6]

hǎn
call, cry, to shout

Rad: 口   Str: 12

| 喊 | **hǎn** | shout, cry out, call sb [5] |

hàn
regret

Rad: 忄   Str: 16

| 遗憾 | **yíhàn** | pity, regret [5] |

háo
grand, heroic

Rad: 豕   Str: 14

豪华	**háohuá**	luxurious [5]
自豪	**zìháo**	to be proud of sth (in a good way), feel a sense of pride [5]
豪迈	**háomài**	heroic, bold [6]

háo
hair, drawing brush, (in the) least, one thousandth

Rad: 毛   Str: 11

丝毫	**sīháo**	very little, of the slightest amount or degree [5]
毫米	**háomǐ**	millimetre [6]
毫无	**háowú**	not in the least, none whatsoever, completely without [6]

Additional words
毫不 **háobù** (not at all).

hé
nuclear, atomic, stone (of fruit)

Rad: 木   Str: 10

| 核心 | **héxīn** | nucleus, core, kernel [5] |
| 考核 | **kǎohé** | examine, assess [6] |

Additional words
核聚变 **héjùbiàn** (nuclear fusion);
核桃 **hétao** (walnut).

hèn
to hate

Rad: 忄   Str: 9

恨	**hèn**	hate [5]
恨不得	**hènbude**	hate that one cannot, really want to [6]
悔恨	**huǐhèn**	regret, lament [6]

héng
to weigh, weight, measure

Rad: 彳   Str: 16

| 平衡 | **pínghéng** | balanced, balance, equilibrium [5] |
| 权衡 | **quánhéng** | to weigh, balance, weigh up [6] |

hóng
rainbow, rainbow

Rad: 虫   Str: 9

| 彩虹 | **cǎihóng** | rainbow [5] |

猴 hóu
monkey

Rad: 犭   Str: 12

| 猴子 | **hóuzi** | monkey [5] |

忽 hū
suddenly

Rad: 心   Str: 8

忽然	**hūrán**	suddenly, all of a sudden [5]
忽视	**hūshì**	to ignore, overlook, neglect [5]
忽略	**hūlüè**	ignore, overlook [6]
疏忽	**shūhu**	to neglect, overlook, carelessness [6]

胡 hú
beard, moustache, aimlessly

Rad: 月   Str: 9

胡说	**húshuō**	talk nonsense, drivel [5]
胡同	**hútòng**	alley, lane [5]
胡乱	**húluàn**	aimlessly, casually [6]
胡须	**húxū**	beard [6]

壶 hú
pot, measure word (for bottle liquid)

Rad: 士   Str: 10

| 壶 | **hú** | pot, measure word (for bottled liquid) [5] |

蝴

hú
butterfly

Rad: 虫   Str: 15

| 蝴蝶 | **húdié** | butterfly [5] |

糊

hú
muddled

Rad: 米   Str: 15

糊涂	**hútu**	muddled, confused, bewildered [5]
模糊	**móhu**	blurred, indistinct, dim, vague, unclear [5]
含糊	**hánhu**	ambiguous, vague, unsure, careless, perfunctory [6]

华

huá
China (abbreviation), magnificent, splendid, flowery

Rad: 十   Str: 6

豪华	**háohuá**	luxurious [5]
华裔	**huáyì**	ethnic Chinese, non-Chinese citizen of Chinese ancestry [5]
繁华	**fánhuá**	flourishing, bustling [6]
华丽	**huálì**	magnificent, gorgeous [6]
华侨	**huáqiáo**	overseas Chinese [6]
精华	**jīnghuá**	best feature, most important part of an object, quintessence, essence, soul [6]

滑

huá
slippery, smooth, cunning

Rad: 氵   Str: 12

| 光滑 | **guānghuá** | smooth, sleek, glossy, slippery [5] |
| 滑 | **huá** | slippery, smooth [5] |

Additional words
滑冰 **huábīng** (ice-skate).

huá
sly

Rad: 犭   Str: 12

狡猾	**jiǎohuá**	sly, cunning, tricky, foxy, crafty [5]

huǎn
slow, sluggish, gradual, to postpone

Rad: 纟   Str: 12

缓解	**huǎnjiě**	ease, relieve (e.g. a crisis) [5]
迟缓	**chíhuǎn**	sluggish, slow [6]
缓和	**huǎnhé**	assuage, ease up, mitigated, relaxed [6]
刻不容缓	**kèbù rónghuǎn**	instant, immediate, or great urgency [6]

huàn
fantasy

Rad: 幺   Str: 4

幻想	**huànxiǎng**	to fantasise, dream, fancy, fantasy, illusion [5]

Additional words
科幻小说 **kēhuàn xiàoshuō** (science fiction novel).

huāng
nervous

Rad: 忄   Str: 12

慌张	**huāngzhāng**	confused, flustered [5]

Additional words
慌忙 **huāngmáng** (in a great rush).

灰 huī
gray, ash

Rad: 火   Str: 6

灰	**huī**	grey, ash [5]
灰尘	**huīchén**	dust [5]
灰心	**huīxīn**	lose heart, be disheartened, be discouraged [5]

挥 huī
scatter, wield, wipe away

Rad: 扌   Str: 9

发挥	**fāhuī**	to bring out implicit or innate qualities, to express (a thought or moral), to develop (an idea), to elaborate (on a theme) [5]
挥	**huī**	to brandish, wipe away, scatter [5]
指挥	**zhǐhuī**	to conduct, to command, to direct, conductor (of an orchestra) [5]
挥霍	**huīhuò**	to squander (money), extravagant [6]

Additional words
挥手 **huīshǒu** (wave).

恢 huī
to restore, to recover, great

Rad: 忄   Str: 9

| 恢复 | **huīfù** | to resume, renew, recover, restore [5] |

汇 huì
remit, to converge (of rivers), to exchange, class, collection

Rad: 氵   Str: 5

词汇	**cíhuì**	vocabulary, list of words (e.g. for language teaching) [5]
汇率	**huìlǜ**	exchange rate [5]
汇报	**huìbào**	to report, to give an account of, to collect information and report back [6]

慧

huì
intelligent

Rad: 心   Str: 15

| 智慧 | **zhìhuì** | wisdom, knowledge, intelligence, intelligent [5] |

惠

huì
favor, kind act (from above)

Rad: 心   Str: 12

优惠	**yōuhuì**	preferential, favourable [5]
实惠	**shíhuì**	tangible benefit, material advantages, advantageous (deal), substantial (discount) [6]
贤惠	**xiánhuì**	virtuous [6]

jī
muscle

Rad: 月   Str: 6

| 肌肉 | **jīròu** | muscle [5] |

击

jī
to hit, to strike, to break

Rad: 凵   Str: 5

射击	**shèjī**	to shoot, to fire (a gun) [5]
冲击	**chōngjī**	impact, shock, pound, attack [6]
打击	**dǎjī**	to hit, to strike, to attack [6]
攻击	**gōngjī**	to attack, to accuse, to charge, an attack (terrorist or military) [6]
袭击	**xíjī**	an attack (esp. surprise attack), raid, to attack [6]

jí
to gather, to collect,
collected works

Rad: 佳   Str: 12

集合	**jíhé**	to gather, assemble [5]
集体	**jítǐ**	collective [5]
集中	**jízhōng**	focus, concentrate, amass, centralised [5]
采集	**cǎijí**	to gather, to collect, to harvest [6]
集团	**jítuán**	group, bloc [6]

Additional words
搜集 **sōují** (collect).

jí
gather up, collect, edit,
compile

Rad: 车   Str: 13

| 编辑 | **biānjí** | edit, compile, editor, compiler [5] |
| 逻辑 | **luóji** | logic (loan word) [5] |

jǐ
crowded, to squeeze

Rad: 扌   Str: 9

| 拥挤 | **yōngjǐ** | push, squeeze, press, shove [5] |

jì
lonesome

Rad: 宀   Str: 11

| 寂寞 | **jìmò** | lonely, lonesome, quiet, still, silent [5] |
| 寂静 | **jìjìng** | silence, quiet (place) [6] |

迹 jì
footprint, mark, trace, vestige, sign, indication, trace

Rad: 辶 Str: 9

名胜古迹	míngshèng gǔjì	place of historical interest [5]
奇迹	qíjì	miracle, marvel, wonder [5]
痕迹	hénjì	trail, mark, trace, vestige [6]
迹象	jìxiàng	mark, indication, sign, indicator [6]
事迹	shìjì	praiseworthy act, deed, achievement, merit [6]
踪迹	zōngjì	trail, trace, tracks, footprints [6]

夹 jiā
clip, folder, to press from both sides, to place in between, narrow lane

Rad: 大 Str: 6

| 夹子 | jiāzi | clamp, clip, tongs, folder, wallet [5] |
| 夹杂 | jiāzá | to mix together, mingle [6] |

嘉 jiā
excellent

Rad: 口 Str: 14

| 嘉宾 | jiābīn | honoured guest [5] |

甲 jiǎ
first in order, first heavenly stem, A (in a sequence of examples involving "A", "B", "C", etc.), armour

Rad: 田 Str: 5

| 甲 | jiǎ | the first of the ten Heavenly Stems, first [5] |
| 指甲 | zhǐjia | fingernail [6] |

驾 jià
to drive, to draw, to harness, to mount

Rad: 马   Str: 8

| 驾驶 | **jiàshǐ** | drive, pilot, steer, navigate [5] |
| 劳驾 | **láojià** | excuse me, may I trouble you [5] |

嫁 jià
marry (a husband)

Rad: 女   Str: 13

| 嫁 | **jià** | take as a husband, marry (a man), shift (blame) [5] |

Additional words
陪嫁 **péijià** (dowry).

jià
to support, frame, rack, framework, measure word (for planes, large vehicles, radios, etc.)

Rad: 木   Str: 9

吵架	**chǎojià**	to quarrel, argue [5]
书架	**shūjià**	bookshelf [5]
绑架	**bǎngjià**	to kidnap, abduct, hijack [6]
打架	**dǎjià**	to fight, to scuffle, to come to blows [6]
框架	**kuàngjià**	frame, framework, outline [6]

Additional words
一架飞机 **yí jià fēijī** (an aeroplane).

肩 jiān
shoulder

Rad: 月   Str: 8

| 肩膀 | **jiānbǎng** | shoulder [5] |

Additional words
肩负 **jiānfù** (take on).

jiān
difficult, hard, hardship

Rad: 艮   Str: 8

艰巨	**jiānjù**	arduous, hard, formidable [5]
艰苦	**jiānkǔ**	difficult, hard, tough [5]
艰难	**jiānnán**	hard, difficult, arduous [6]

兼

jiān
double, twice, simultaneous, holding two or more (official) posts at the same time

Rad: 丷   Str: 10

| 兼职 | **jiānzhí** | part-time job, second job [5] |
| 统筹兼顾 | **tǒngchóu jiāngù** | overall plan taking all factors into account [6] |

<u>Additional words</u>
兼容 **jiānróng** (compatible).

jiǎn
pick up, collect, gather

Rad: 扌   Str: 10

| 捡 | **jiǎn** | pick up, collect, gather [5] |

剪

jiǎn
scissors, cut with scissors

Rad: 刀   Str: 11

| 剪刀 | **jiǎndāo** | scissors [5] |
| 剪彩 | **jiǎncǎi** | cut the ribbon (at an opening ceremony) [6] |

jiàn
fulfill (a promise), tread, walk

Rad: 足   Str: 12

实践	**shíjiàn**	to practice, to put into practice, to fulfil [5]
践踏	**jiàntà**	to trample [6]

jiàn
recommend (a person)

Rad: 艹   Str: 9

推荐	**tuījiàn**	recommend [5]

jiàn
gradual, gradually

Rad: 氵   Str: 11

逐渐	**zhújiàn**	gradually, by degrees [5]
循序渐进	**xúnxù jiànjìn**	in sequence, step by step, to make steady progress incrementally [6]

jiàng
sauce, jam

Rad: 酉   Str: 13

酱油	**jiàngyóu**	soy sauce [5]

jiāo
to water

Rad: 氵   Str: 9

浇   **jiāo**   water, irrigate, pour, sprinkle, cast [5]

jiāo
glue, gum

Rad: 月   Str: 10

胶水   **jiāoshuǐ**   glue (water-based) [5]

Additional words
橡胶 **xiàngjiāo** (rubber).

jiāo
pepper

Rad: 木   Str: 12

辣椒   **làjiāo**   hot pepper, chilli, chilli pepper [5]

jiǎo
crafty, cunning, sly

Rad: 犭   Str: 9

狡猾   **jiǎohuá**   sly, cunning, tricky, foxy, crafty [5]

jiē
rank, step, stairs

Rad: 阝   Str: 6

阶段	**jiēduàn**	stage, phase [5]
台阶	**táijiē**	flight of steps (leading up to a house), step (over obstacle), bench, way out of an embarrassing situation [5]
阶层	**jiēcéng**	social stratum [6]

Additional words
阶级 **jiējí** (social class, steps, stairs, rank).

jú
tangerine

Rad: 木   Str: 10

| 桔子 | **júzi** | orange, tangerine [5] |

jiè
swear off, warn against

Rad: 戈   Str: 7

戒	**jiè**	swear off, warn against [5]
戒指	**jièzhi**	ring (on a finger) [5]
戒备	**jièbèi**	to guard against, watch out for [6]

Additional words
戒严 **jièyán** (enforce martial law).

jiè
arrive at (place or time), period, to become due, measure word (for events, meetings, elections)

Rad: 尸   Str: 8

| 届 | **jiè** | period, session, to arrive at (place or time), measure word (for events, meetings etc.) [5] |

jǐn
cautious

Rad: 讠   Str: 13

| 谨慎 | **jǐnshèn** | cautious, prudent, circumspect, careful, mindful [5] |

jìn
strength, stalwart, sturdy

Rad: 力   Str: 7

| 使劲儿 | **shǐjìnr** | keep at it, give everything one has [5] |
| 干劲 | **gànjìn** | vigour, drive, enthusiasm, energy [6] |

jìng
to respect, to venerate, to salute, to offer

Rad: 攵   Str: 12

尊敬	**zūnjìng**	respect, esteem [5]
崇敬	**chóngjìng**	respect, revere [6]
恭敬	**gōngjìng**	dutiful, respectful [6]
敬礼	**jìnglǐ**	salute [6]
敬业	**jìngyè**	dedicate oneself to one's job [6]

jiù
to save, to assist, to rescue

Rad: 攵   Str: 11

救	**jiù**	to rescue, save, assist [5]
救护车	**jiùhùchē**	ambulance [5]
补救	**bǔjiù**	repair, remedy [6]
救济	**jiùjì**	emergency relief, to help disaster victims [6]
抢救	**qiǎngjiù**	rescue, save [6]
挽救	**wǎnjiù**	to save, rescue, remedy [6]

Additional words
救命 **jiùmìng** (Help! Save me!).

jiù
maternal uncle

Rad: 臼   Str: 13

舅舅   **jiùjiu**   mother's brother, maternal uncle [5]

矩
jǔ
carpenter's square, rule

Rad: 矢   Str: 9

规矩   **guīju**   rule, manner, custom, decent, conforming to norms [5]

Additional words
矩阵 **jǔzhèn** (matrix).

jù
very large, huge, tremendous, gigantic

Rad: 工   Str: 4

艰巨   **jiānjù**   arduous, hard, formidable [5]
巨大   **jùdà**   huge, enormous [5]

俱
jù
entirely, without exception, a social club

Rad: 亻   Str: 10

俱乐部   **jùlèbù**   club (i.e. a group or organization) [5]
与日俱增   **yǔrìjùzēng**   to increase steadily, to grow with each passing day [6]

juān
to donate, to contribute

Rad: 扌   Str: 10

| 捐 | **juān** | donate [5] |

---

juǎn
to roll (up), to sweep up, to carry on, coil

juàn
volume, book, exam paper

Rad: 厄   Str: 8

| 试卷 | **shìjuàn** | examination paper [5] |
| 卷 | **juǎn** | to roll (up), to sweep up, to carry on, coil, to roll, chapter, examination paper [6] |

Additional words
春卷 **chūnjuǎn** (spring roll).

jūn
army, military, arms, troops

Rad: 冖   Str: 6

冠军	**guànjūn**	champion [5]
军事	**jūnshì**	military affairs [5]
季军	**jìjūn**	third place, bronze medallist [6]
将军	**jiāngjūn**	general (in the army) [6]
军队	**jūnduì**	army troops [6]
亚军	**yàjūn**	second place (in a contest), runner-up [6]

Additional words
敌军 **díjūn** (enemy troops).

jūn
equal, even, all, uniform

Rad: 土   Str: 7

| 均匀 | **jūnyún** | even, uniform, well-distributed [5] |
| 平均 | **píngjūn** | average, mathematical mean [5] |

jùn
smart, eminent, handsome, talented

Rad: 亻   Str: 9

| 英俊 | **yīngjùn** | handsome [5] |

kǎn
to chop

Rad: 石   Str: 9

| 砍 | **kǎn** | chop, cut [5] |
| 砍伐 | **kǎnfá** | hew, cut, lumber [6] |

Additional words
砍柴 **kǎnchái** (cut firewood).

kào
depend upon, lean on, near, by, against, to support

Rad: 非   Str: 15

靠	**kào**	to lean on, support, against, by [5]
可靠	**kěkào**	reliable, dependable [5]
靠拢	**kàolǒng**	to bring to a close [6]
依靠	**yīkào**	rely on, depend on, backing, support [6]

kē
grain, measure word (for small spheres, pearls, corn grains, teeth, hearts)

Rad: 页   Str: 14

| 颗 | **kē** | grain, measure word (for small spheres, pearls, corn grains, teeth, hearts) [5] |

Additional words
一颗珠子 **yì kē zhūzi** (one pearl).

kěn
earnest

Rad: 心   Str: 10

| 诚恳 | **chéngkěn** | honest, sincere [5] |
| 恳切 | **kěnqiè** | earnest, sincere [6] |

Additional words
恳求 **kěnqiú** (plead).

控 kòng
to accuse, to charge, to control, to sue

Rad: 扌   Str: 11

| 控制 | **kòngzhì** | to control, dominate, command [5] |
| 遥控 | **yáokòng** | remote control [6] |

kù
warehouse, storehouse

Rad: 广   Str: 7

| 车库 | **chēkù** | garage, hanger [5] |
| 仓库 | **cāngkù** | storehouse, warehouse, depot [6] |

Additional words
数据库 **shùjùkù** (database).

夸 kuā
to boast

Rad: 大   Str: 6

| 夸 | **kuā** | praise, laud, commend, overstate, exaggerate, boast [5] |
| 夸张 | **kuāzhāng** | praise, laud, commend, overstate, exaggerate, boast [5] |

Additional words
夸大 **kuādà** (exaggerate).

kuān
lenient, wide, broad

Rad: 宀   Str: 10

宽	**kuān**	wide, broad [5]
宽敞	**kuānchang**	spacious, roominess [6]
宽容	**kuānróng**	lenient, tolerant [6]

kuáng
conceited, mad

Rad: 犭   Str: 7

疯狂	**fēngkuáng**	crazy, maniac, mad, wild, frenzied, unbridled [5]

Additional words
妄想狂 **wàngxiǎngkuáng** (paranoia).

kuī
deficiency, deficit

Rad: 二   Str: 3

吃亏	**chīkuī**	suffer losses, be in an unfavourable situation [5]
多亏	**duōkuī**	be lucky to, it is fortunate that, thanks to, luckily [5]
幸亏	**xìngkuī**	luckily, fortunately [5]
亏待	**kuīdài**	treat unfairly [6]
亏损	**kuīsǔn**	deficit, financial loss [6]

kuì
ashamed

Rad: 忄   Str: 12

惭愧	**cánkuì**	ashamed [5]
不愧	**búkuì**	be worthy of, deserve to be called, prove oneself to be, creditably [6]

Additional words
羞愧 **xiūkuì** (feel ashamed).

kūn

descendant, elder brother

Rad: 日　Str: 8

| 昆虫 | **kūnchóng** | insect [5] |

<u>Additional words</u>
昆明 **kūnmíng** (Kunming (city)).

kuò

enlarge

Rad: 扌　Str: 6

扩大	**kuòdà**	enlarge, expand, extend [5]
扩充	**kuòchōng**	extend, enlarge [6]
扩散	**kuòsàn**	to diffuse, spread, diffusion [6]
扩张	**kuòzhāng**	expansion, dilation, to expand (e.g. one's power or influence), to broaden [6]

kuò

enclose, include

Rad: 扌　Str: 9

| 包括 | **bāokuò** | include, consist of, comprise [5] |
| 概括 | **gàikuò** | to summarise, generalise, summary [5] |

lán

cut off, hinder

Rad: 扌　Str: 8

| 拦 | **lán** | cut off, hinder [5] |
| 阻拦 | **zǔlán** | to stop, obstruct [6] |

lǎn
look over, to view

Rad: 见   Str: 9

浏览	**liúlǎn**	browse, skim through [5]
游览	**yóulǎn**	visit, tour, go sightseeing [5]
展览	**zhǎnlǎn**	to put on display, exhibit, show [5]
博览会	**bólǎnhuì**	exhibition [6]

làn
overcooked, rotten, soft

Rad: 火   Str: 9

烂	**làn**	rot, rotten [5]
灿烂	**cànlàn**	bright, splendid, brilliant, magnificent [6]
腐烂	**fǔlàn**	rot, perish [6]

lǎng
clear, bright

Rad: 阝   Str: 10

朗读	**lǎngdú**	to read aloud [5]
开朗	**kāilǎng**	optimistic, cheerful, carefree [6]
晴朗	**qínglǎng**	sunny and cloudless [6]

Additional words
朗讼 **lǎngsòng** (recite).

láo
toil

Rad: 力   Str: 7

劳动	**láodòng**	work, labour [5]
劳驾	**láojià**	excuse me, may I trouble you [5]
疲劳	**píláo**	exhausted, tired [5]
操劳	**cāoláo**	work hard [6]
功劳	**gōngláo**	credit, contribution, outstanding service [6]
勤劳	**qínláo**	hardworking, diligent, industrious, assiduous [6]

lǎo
grandma (maternal), governess, old woman

Rad: 女   Str: 9

| 姥姥 | lǎolao | maternal grandmother, grandma [5] |

léi
thunder

Rad: 雨   Str: 13

| 雷 | léi | thunder [5] |
| 雷达 | léidá | radar (loan word) [6] |

Additional words
雷雨 **léiyǔ** (thunderstorm).

lèi
kind, type, class, category, similar, like, to resemble

Rad: 米   Str: 9

类型	lèixíng	type, category [5]
人类	rénlèi	mankind, humanity, humankind [5]
种类	zhǒnglèi	kind, type, sort, variety [5]
类似	lèisì	similar, analogous [6]

lèi
tears

Rad: 氵   Str: 8

| 流泪 | liúlèi | to cry [5] |
| 热泪盈眶 | rèlèi yíngkuàng | eye's brimming with tears, extremely moved [6] |

Additional words
泪珠 **lèizhū** (teardrop).

厘 lí
one thousandth

Rad: 厂　Str: 9

厘米　**límǐ**　centimetre [5]

梨 lí
pear

Rad: 木　Str: 11

梨　**lí**　pear [5]

璃 lí
colored glaze, glass

Rad: 王　Str: 14

玻璃　**bōli**　glass [5]

Additional words
琉璃 **liúlí** (coloured glaze).

立 lì
to stand, erect, vertical

Rad: 立　Str: 5

成立	**chénglì**	to establish, found [5]
独立	**dúlì**	stand alone, independence [5]
建立	**jiànlì**	build, establish [5]
立即	**lìjí**	immediately, at once [5]
立刻	**lìkè**	immediately, at once, right away [5]
创立	**chuànglì**	found, establish, initiate [6]
对立	**duìlì**	oppose, counter, go against [6]
孤立	**gūlì**	isolated, isolate [6]
立场	**lìchǎng**	position, stand, standpoint [6]
立方	**lìfāng**	cube [6]
立交桥	**lìjiāoqiáo**	overpass [6]
立体	**lìtǐ**	solid, 3D object [6]
立足	**lìzú**	to base oneself on, find a foothold [6]
确立	**quèlì**	to establish [6]
设立	**shèlì**	to set up, establish [6]
树立	**shùlì**	to set up, establish [6]
中立	**zhōnglì**	neutral, neutrality [6]

lián
curtain

Rad: 巾   Str: 8

| 窗帘 | **chuānglián** | window curtain [5] |

liàn
feel attached to, long for, love

Rad: 心   Str: 10

| 恋爱 | **liàn'ài** | in love, romantic love [5] |
| 留恋 | **liúliàn** | be reluctant to leave [6] |

liàn
chain, lead or tin ore

Rad: 钅   Str: 12

| 项链 | **xiàngliàn** | necklace [5] |

Additional words
拉链 **lāliàn** (zip).

liáng
good, very, very much

Rad: 艮   Str: 7

良好	**liánghǎo**	good, favourable, well, fine [5]
善良	**shànliáng**	kind, virtuous [5]
改良	**gǎiliáng**	to improve, better, reform, amend [6]
良心	**liángxīn**	conscience [6]

Additional words
优良 **yōuliáng** (good, fine).

liáng
provisions

Rad: 米　Str: 13

粮食　**liángshi**　grain, food [5]

liáo
to treat, to cure

Rad: 广　Str: 7

治疗　**zhìliáo**　to treat, to cure, medical treatment, cure [5]

Additional words
疗法 **liáofǎ** (therapy).

liè
ardent, intense, split, crack, rend

Rad: 灬　Str: 10

激烈	**jīliè**	intense, fierce [5]
强烈	**qiángliè**	intense, strong, violent [5]
热烈	**rèliè**	warm (welcome etc.), ardent, enthusiastic [5]
剧烈	**jùliè**	acute, violent, severe [6]
猛烈	**měngliè**	fierce, violent, vigorous [6]
兴高采烈	**xìnggāo cǎiliè**	be in high spirits, be enraptured [6]
壮烈	**zhuàngliè**	brave, heroic [6]

Additional words
轰轰烈烈 **hōnghōnglièliè** (grand, spectacular).

liè
inferior

Rad: 力　Str: 6

| 恶劣 | **èliè** | vile, nasty, disgusting [5] |
| 优胜劣汰 | **yōushèng liètài** | survival of the fittest [6] |

lín
to face, to overlook, to arrive, to be (just) about to, just before

Rad: 丨   Str: 9

光临	**guānglín**	Welcome!, You honour us with your presence, It is an honour to have you [5]
临时	**línshí**	temporary [5]
面临	**miànlín**	to be faced with, be confronted with, be up against [5]
濒临	**bīnlín**	on the verge of [6]
降临	**jiànglín**	to befall, become of [6]
临床	**línchuáng**	clinical [6]

Additional words
濒临 **bīnlín** (to be close to (a body of water)).

líng
alert, departed soul, efficacious, quick, effective, intelligence

Rad: 火   Str: 7

灵活	**línghuó**	flexible, agile, nimble [5]
机灵	**jīling**	wise, clever [6]
灵感	**línggǎn**	inspiration, insight, a burst of creativity in scientific or artistic endeavour [6]
灵魂	**línghún**	soul, spirit, conscience [6]
灵敏	**língmǐn**	smart, clever, sensitive, sharp [6]
心灵	**xīnlíng**	heart, soul, psyche [6]

líng
bell

Rad: 钅   Str: 10

铃	**líng**	bell [5]

líng
encroach, soar, thick ice

Rad: 冫   Str: 10

冰激凌	**bīngjīlíng**	ice cream [5]
凌晨	**língchén**	before dawn [6]

lǐng
neck, collar, to lead, to receive

Rad: 页　　Str: 11

本领	**běnlǐng**	skill, ability, capability [5]
系领带	**jìlǐngdài**	to tie a necktie [5]
领导	**lǐngdǎo**	lead, leader, leadership [5]
领域	**lǐngyù**	field, sphere, domain, realm, area, territory [5]
带领	**dàilǐng**	to lead, guide, direct [6]
纲领	**gānglǐng**	guiding principle, program, platform [6]
领会	**lǐnghuì**	understand, comprehend, grasp [6]
领事馆	**lǐngshìguǎn**	consulate [6]
领土	**lǐngtǔ**	territory [6]
领悟	**lǐngwù**	realisation, comprehension [6]
领先	**lǐngxiān**	to lead, to be in front [6]
领袖	**lǐngxiù**	leader [6]
率领	**shuàilǐng**	lead, head, command [6]
占领	**zhànlǐng**	to occupy (a territory), to hold [6]

lìng
cause to be, order, command, decree, honorable

Rad: 人　　Str: 5

命令	**mìnglìng**	command, order [5]
夏令营	**xiàlìngyíng**	summer camp [5]
司令	**sīlìng**	commander, commanding officer [6]
指令	**zhǐlìng**	order, instruction [6]

liú
clear, deep (of water), swift

Rad: 氵　　Str: 9

| 浏览 | **liúlǎn** | browse, skim through [5] |

lóng
dragon, imperial

Rad: 龙   Str: 5

龙	lóng	dragon [5]
水龙头	shuǐlóngtóu	tap, faucet [6]

Additional words
恐龙 **kǒnglóng** (dinosaur);
龙虾 **lóngxiā** (lobster).

lòu
funnel, to leak, to let out, to divulge

Rad: 氵   Str: 14

漏	lòu	to leak, divulge, leave out by mistake [5]
走漏	zǒulòu	to leak (of information, liquid etc), to divulge [6]

lǜ
rate, frequency, to lead, command
shuài
careless

Rad: 玄   Str: 11

汇率	huìlǜ	exchange rate [5]
坦率	tǎnshuài	open, frank, candid [5]
效率	xiàolǜ	efficiency [5]
草率	cǎoshuài	careless, slapdash, cursory [6]
频率	pínlǜ	frequency [6]
率领	shuàilǐng	lead, head, command [6]

lù
shore, land, continent

Rad: 阝   Str: 7

陆地	lùdì	land, dry land [5]
陆续	lùxù	one after another, in succession [5]
登陆	dēnglù	disembark, land, make landfall (of typhoon etc.) [6]

Additional words
大陆 **dàlù** (continent).

74

lù
to record, to hit, to copy

Rad: 彐　Str: 8

记录	jìlù	take notes, record [5]
纪录	jìlù	record, memorial [5]
录取	lùqǔ	to recruit, enrol, matriculate [5]
录音	lùyīn	to record (sound), sound recording [5]
目录	mùlù	catalogue, table of contents, directory (on computer hard drive), list, contents [5]
备忘录	bèiwànglù	note, memo [6]
登录	dēnglù	to register, login [6]

luè
plan, strategy, outline, summary, slightly, rather, to rob, to plunder, to summarize

Rad: 田　Str: 11

省略	shěnglüè	omit, omission [5]
策略	cèlüè	tactic, policy [6]
忽略	hūlüè	ignore, overlook [6]
侵略	qīnlüè	invasion [6]
战略	zhànluè	strategy [6]

Additional words
略微 lüèwēi (slightly).

lún
wheel, gear, (by) turn, rotate

Rad: 车　Str: 8

轮流	lúnliú	to alternate, take turns [5]
轮船	lúnchuán	steamship, ship [6]
轮廓	lúnkuò	outline, contour, profile, silhouette, general situation [6]
轮胎	lúntāi	tyre [6]

luó
logic, patrol

Rad: 辶　Str: 11

逻辑	luóji	logic (loan word) [5]
巡逻	xúnluó	to patrol (police, army, navy) [6]

luò
small net, net-like

Rad: 纟   Str: 9

网络	**wǎngluò**	network (computing, telecommunications, transport etc.), internet [5]
联络	**liánluò**	communication, to get in touch with, to contact [6]
络绎不绝	**luòyìbùjué**	in an endless stream [6]

mà
scold, abuse

Rad: 马   Str: 9

骂	**mà**	to scold, abuse, curse [5]

mài
wheat, barley, oats

Rad: 麦   Str: 7

麦克风	**màikèfēng**	microphone (loan word) [5]
小麦	**xiǎomài**	wheat [5]

Additional words
麦片 **màipiàn** (oatmeal).

mán
steamed bread

Rad: 饣   Str: 14

馒头	**mántou**	steamed bun [5]

máo
spear, lance, pike

Rad: 矛   Str: 5

矛盾   **máodùn**   contradiction, contradictory (lit. spear-shield) [5]

máo
fashionable, mane, bang (hair)

Rad: 髟   Str: 14

时髦   **shímáo**   in fashion [5]

mào
commerce, trade

Rad: 贝   Str: 9

贸易   **màoyì**   trade [5]

méi
eyebrow, upper margin

Rad: 目   Str: 9

眉毛   **méimao**   eyebrow, brow [5]

Additional words
眉头 **méitóu** (brows).

媒

méi
medium, intermediary, matchmaker, go-between

Rad: 女   Str: 12

| 媒体 | **méitǐ** | media (esp. news media) [5] |
| 媒介 | **méijiè** | agent, medium, intermediary [6] |

煤

méi
coal

Rad: 火   Str: 13

| 煤炭 | **méitàn** | coal [5] |

Additional words
煤油 **méiyóu** (kerosene).

霉

méi
bacteria, fungi, moldy

Rad: 雨   Str: 15

| 倒霉 | **dǎoméi** | be unlucky, have bad luck [5] |

魅

mèi
demon, magic, to charm

Rad: 鬼   Str: 14

| 魅力 | **mèilì** | glamour, charm [5] |

mì
secret

Rad: 禾   Str: 10

秘密	**mìmì**	secret [5]
秘书	**mìshū**	secretary [5]
神秘	**shénmì**	mysterious, mystical [5]
奥秘	**àomì**	mystery, enigma [6]

mì
honey

Rad: 虫   Str: 14

| 蜜蜂 | **mìfēng** | bee, honeybee [5] |

mián
sleep

Rad: 目   Str: 10

| 失眠 | **shīmián** | to be unable to sleep, suffer from insomnia [5] |

Additional words
冬眠 **dōngmián** (to hibernate, hibernation).

miáo
sprout, Miao tribe

Rad: 艹   Str: 8

| 苗条 | **miáotiao** | slim, slender, graceful [5] |
| 拔苗助长 | **bámiáo zhùzhǎng** | over-zealous [6] |

Additional words
禾苗 **hémiáo** (seedlings);
火苗 **huǒmiáo** (flame).

miáo
depict, to trace (a drawing), to copy, to touch up

Rad: 扌 Str: 11

| 描写 | **miáoxiě** | portray, depict, describe [5] |
| 描绘 | **miáohuì** | describe, portray [6] |

Additional words
描述 **miáoshù** (describe).

miào
clever, wonderful

Rad: 女 Str: 7

巧妙	**qiǎomiào**	clever, ingenious [5]
美妙	**měimiào**	beautiful (e.g. work of art), wonderful, splendid [6]
莫名其妙	**mòmíng qímiào**	unfathomable mystery, unable to make head or tail of it [6]
奇妙	**qímiào**	wonderful [6]

Additional words
奥妙 **àomiào** (profound, secret).

mǐn
keen

Rad: 攵 Str: 11

过敏	**guòmǐn**	allergy, be allergic to [5]
敏感	**mǐngǎn**	sensitive, susceptible [5]
灵敏	**língmǐn**	smart, clever, sensitive, sharp [6]
敏捷	**mǐnjié**	quick, nimble, agile [6]
敏锐	**mǐnruì**	keen, subtitle, acute, brisk [6]

mō
feel with the hand, to touch, to stroke, to grope, to feel (one's pulse), imitate, copy

Rad: 扌 Str: 13

摸	**mō**	feel with the hand, to touch, to stroke, to grope, to feel (one's pulse), imitate, copy [5]
抚摸	**fǔmō**	to stroke, rub, caress [6]
摸索	**mōsuǒ**	to feel about, grope, fumble, do things slowly [6]

模

mó
imitate, model, norm, pattern

mú
appearance

Rad: 木　Str: 14

规模	**guīmó**	scale, scope, extent [5]
模仿	**mófǎng**	copy, imitate [5]
模糊	**móhu**	blurred, indistinct, dim, vague, unclear [5]
模特	**mótè**	fashion model [5]
模范	**mófàn**	model, fine example [6]
模式	**móshì**	mode, style [6]
模型	**móxíng**	model, mould, matrix, pattern, die [6]
模样	**múyàng**	appearance, look [6]

摩

mó
rub

Rad: 手　Str: 15

摩托车	**mótuōchē**	motorcycle, motorbike [5]
按摩	**ànmó**	massage [6]
摩擦	**mócā**	rub, scrape, friction [6]

陌

mò
raised path, street

Rad: 阝　Str: 8

陌生	**mòshēng**	strange, unfamiliar [5]

Additional words
陌生人 **mòshēngrén** (stranger).

漠

mò
desert, unconcerned

Rad: 氵　Str: 13

沙漠	**shāmò**	desert [5]

Additional words
漠然 **mòrán** (apathetically).

mò
lonesome

Rad: 宀　Str: 13

寂寞　**jìmò**　lonely, lonesome, quiet, still, silent [5]

mǒu
some, (a) certain (used before measure word and noun)

Rad: 木　Str: 9

某　**mǒu**　certain, some [5]

Additional words
某人 **mǒurén** (somebody).

mù
tree, wood

Rad: 木　Str: 4

木头　**mùtou**　slow-witted, blockhead, log (of wood, timber etc.) [5]

麻木　**mámù**　numb [6]

Additional words
乔木 **qiáomù** (arbour).

mù
stage curtain, tent

Rad: 巾　Str: 13

开幕式　**kāimùshì**　opening ceremony [5]
字幕　**zìmù**　caption, subtitle [5]

内幕　**nèimù**　inside story, low-down [6]
屏幕　**píngmù**　viewing screen [6]

纳 nà
to accept, to pay (tax etc.)

Rad: 纟   Str: 7

归纳	**guīnà**	conclude [5]
采纳	**cǎinà**	to accept [6]
缴纳	**jiǎonà**	to contribute, pay (taxes etc.) [6]
纳闷儿	**nàmènr**	feel puzzled [6]
容纳	**róngnà**	to accommodate, contain, hold [6]

奈 nài
how can one help

Rad: 大   Str: 8

| 无奈 | **wúnài** | have no alternative (abbr. for 无可奈何 wúkěnàihé) [5] |

<u>Additional words</u>
无可奈何 **wúkěnàihé** (have no alternative).

嫩 nèn
tender, soft

Rad: 女   Str: 14

| 嫩 | **nèn** | tender, delicate, rare, underdone, light, pale, callow [5] |

<u>Additional words</u>
娇嫩 **jiāonèn** (tender and lovely).

嗯 ńg
huh (interjection)

Rad: 口   Str: 13

<u>Notes</u>
Also pronounced **èn** (O.K., Agreed!).

| 嗯 | **ńg** | huh (interjection) [5] |

niàn
read aloud, to read aloud

Rad: 心　　Str: 8

niáng
mother, young lady

Rad: 女　　Str: 10

概念	**gàiniàn**	concept, idea, conception [5]
观念	**guānniàn**	concept, idea, thought, sense, ideology [5]
怀念	**huáiniàn**	cherish the memory of, think of, miss [5]
纪念	**jìniàn**	commemorate, commemoration, memento [5]
念	**niàn**	read aloud, study, attend school [5]
想念	**xiǎngniàn**	to remember with longing, miss [5]
留念	**liúniàn**	accept or keep as souvenir [6]
思念	**sīniàn**	miss, think of, long for [6]
信念	**xìnniàn**	belief, faith, conviction [6]
悬念	**xuánniàn**	suspense (in a movie, play etc.), concern for sb's welfare [6]

| 姑娘 | **gūniang** | girl, young woman, daughter [5] |
| 新娘 | **xīnniáng** | bride [6] |

nìng
peaceful, rather

níng
tranquil

Rad: 宀　　Str: 5

宁可	**nìngkě**	would rather [5]
安宁	**ānníng**	peaceful, calm [6]
宁肯	**nìngkěn**	would rather, it would be better [6]
宁愿	**nìngyuàn**	would rather [6]

Additional words
辽宁 **Liáoníng** (Liaoning (a province)).

nóng
agriculture

Rad: 冖　　Str: 6

农村	**nóngcūn**	rural area, countryside, village [5]
农民	**nóngmín**	peasant [5]
农业	**nóngyè**	agriculture, farming [5]
农历	**nónglì**	traditional lunar calendar [6]

nóng
concentrated, dense

Rad: 氵　　Str: 9

| 浓 | **nóng** | dense, thick [5] |
| 浓厚 | **nónghòu** | dense, thick (fog, clouds etc.), to have a strong interest in, saturated (colour) [6] |

Additional words
浓度 **nóngdù** (consistency).

ōu
Europe

Rad: 欠　　Str: 8

| 欧洲 | **ōuzhōu** | Europe, European [5] |

Additional words
欧姆 **ōumǔ** (ohm).

pāi
to clap, to pat, to beat, to hit, to slap, to take (a picture)

Rad: 扌　　Str: 8

| 拍 | **pāi** | to pat, clap, racket, to take a photograph [5] |

Additional words
拍摄 **pāishè** (take a picture);
乒乓拍 **pīngpāngpāi** (ping-pong paddle).

pài
clique, school, group, faction, to dispatch

Rad: 氵   Str: 9

派	**pài**	send, appoint, clique, faction, pi (Greek letter) [5]
派别	**pàibié**	faction, group [6]
派遣	**pàiqiǎn**	send, dispatch [6]

Additional words
党派 **dǎngpài** (political parties).

盼

pàn
to hope for, to long for, to expect

Rad: 目   Str: 9

| 盼望 | **pànwàng** | to hope for, look forward to [5] |

炮

pào
cannon, gun, firecracker

Rad: 火   Str: 9

| 鞭炮 | **biānpào** | firecrackers [5] |

Additional words
炮弹 **pàodàn** (shell).

péi
to cultivate, to earth up

Rad: 土   Str: 11

培训	**péixùn**	to cultivate, train [5]
培养	**péiyǎng**	to train, develop, groom (for a position) [5]
培育	**péiyù**	to cultivate, nurture, breed [6]
栽培	**zāipéi**	grow, cultivate [6]

賠 **péi**
lose in trade, pay damage

Rad: 贝　Str: 12

| 賠偿 | **péicháng** | to compensate [5] |

Additional words
赔不是 **péibùshi** (apologize).

佩 **pèi**
to respect

Rad: 亻　Str: 8

| 佩服 | **pèifu** | to admire [5] |
| 钦佩 | **qīnpèi** | admire, look up to [6] |

配 **pèi**
to join, to fit, to mate, to mix, to match, to deserve

Rad: 酉　Str: 10

分配	**fēnpèi**	to assign, allocate, distribute [5]
配合	**pèihé**	matching, fitting in with, compatible with, to correspond, to fit, to conform to, to cooperate [5]
搭配	**dāpèi**	to pair, match, arrange (in pairs) [6]
配备	**pèibèi**	to allocate, to provide, to outfit with [6]
配偶	**pèi'ǒu**	consort, mate [6]
配套	**pèitào**	form a complete set [6]
支配	**zhīpèi**	control, dominate, arrange [6]

喷 **pēn**
to puff, to spout, to spray, to spurt, fragrant, sneeze

Rad: 口　Str: 12

| 打喷嚏 | **dǎpēntì** | to sneeze [5] |

pén
basin

Rad: 皿　Str: 9

| 盆 | **pén** | basin, tub, pot [5] |
| 盆地 | **péndì** | basin (of land) [6] |

碰

pèng
to touch, to meet with,
to bump

Rad: 石　Str: 13

| 碰 | **pèng** | touch, bump, meet, run into [5] |

Additional words
碰见 **pèngjiàn** (happen to meet).

pī
scatter, separate, to open,
to unroll, to spread out

Rad: 扌　Str: 8

| 披 | **pī** | drape over one's shoulder [5] |

疲

pí
weary

Rad: 疒　Str: 10

疲劳	**píláo**	exhausted, tired [5]
疲惫	**píbèi**	tired out, exhausted [6]
疲倦	**píjuàn**	tired and sleepy, weary, fatigued [6]

Additional words
疲乏 **pífá** (tired).

pǐ
mate, one of a pair, measure word (for horses, mules, bolts of cloth)

Rad: 匚   Str: 4

| 匹 | pǐ | measure word (for horses, mules, cloth) [5] |

Additional words
三匹马 **sān pǐ mǎ** (three horses).

piāo
to float

Rad: 风   Str: 15

| 飘 | piāo | to float [5] |
| 飘扬 | piāoyáng | wave, flutter, fly [6] |

pīn
piece together, stake (all), spell, join together

Rad: 扌   Str: 9

拼音	pīnyīn	pinyin (Romanisation of Chinese) [5]
拼搏	pīnbó	go all out in work [6]
拼命	pīnmìng	to be ready to risk one's life (in fighting, work, etc.), bend over backwards, do one's utmost [6]

pín
frequency, frequently, repetitious

Rad: 页   Str: 13

频道	píndào	channel (TV), frequency [5]
频繁	pínfán	often, frequently [6]
频率	pínlǜ	frequency [6]
视频	shìpín	video [6]

pǐn
conduct, grade, thing, product, good

Rad: 口   Str: 9

产品	**chǎnpǐn**	goods, merchandise, product [5]
日用品	**rìyòngpǐn**	daily necessaries [5]
商品	**shāngpǐn**	commodity, goods [5]
作品	**zuòpǐn**	works (of literature and art) [5]
次品	**cìpǐn**	defective goods [6]
毒品	**dúpǐn**	drugs, narcotics, poison [6]
工艺品	**gōngyìpǐn**	handicraft [6]
品尝	**pǐncháng**	to taste a small amount, to sample [6]
品德	**pǐndé**	moral character [6]
品质	**pǐnzhì**	character, quality (of a person, product etc.) [6]
品种	**pǐnzhǒng**	breed, variety [6]
样品	**yàngpǐn**	sample [6]

píng
lean against, proof, to rely on, to depend on, to be based on

Rad: 几   Str: 8

| 凭 | **píng** | rely on, depend on, lean on [5] |
| 文凭 | **wénpíng** | diploma [6] |

pó
grandmother, matron, mother-in-law

Rad: 女   Str: 11

| 老婆 | **lǎopo** | wife [5] |

pò
to force, to compel,
pressing, urgent

Rad: 辶　Str: 8

迫切	**pòqiè**	pressing, urgent [5]
逼迫	**bīpò**	force, compel [6]
紧迫	**jǐnpò**	urgent [6]
迫不及待	**pòbù jídài**	can't wait (for), be really excited about [6]
迫害	**pòhài**	persecute, treat sb. with cruelty, oppress cruelly [6]
强迫	**qiǎngpò**	to force, compel, coerce [6]
压迫	**yāpò**	oppress, repress, stress (physics) [6]

qí
even, to make even

Rad: 齐　Str: 6

整齐	**zhěngqí**	in good order, neat, tidy [5]
齐全	**qíquán**	complete, all ready [6]
齐心协力	**qíxīn xiélì**	to work with a common purpose, to make concerted efforts, to pull together, to work as one [6]

Additional words
一齐 **yìqí** (together).

qí
chess

Rad: 木　Str: 12

象棋	**xiàngqí**	Chinese chess [5]

Additional words
围棋 **wéiqí** (Go (game)).

qǐ
plan a project, stand on
tiptoe

Rad: 人　Str: 6

企业	**qǐyè**	enterprise, business [5]
企图	**qǐtú**	try, attempt [6]

Additional words
企鹅 **qǐ'é** (penguin).

启 qǐ
to open, to start

Rad: 口   Str: 7

启发	qǐfā	to enlighten, to explain and arouse interest, to inspire, inspiration [5]
启程	qǐchéng	to set out on a journey [6]
启蒙	qǐméng	introduction, initiation, enlightenment [6]
启事	qǐshì	announcement, notice [6]
启示	qǐshì	enlightenment, revelation, apocalypse [6]

器 qì
device, tool, utensil

Rad: 口   Str: 16

充电器	chōngdiànqì	electric charger [5]
机器	jīqì	machine [5]
乐器	yuèqì	musical instrument [5]
器材	qìcái	equipment, material [6]
器官	qìguān	organ (part of body tissue), apparatus [6]
容器	róngqì	container, vessel [6]
武器	wǔqì	weapon, arms [6]
仪器	yíqì	instrument, apparatus [6]

Additional words
祭器 jìqì (sacrificial utensil);
器械 qìxiè (apparatus).

谦 qiān
modest

Rad: 讠   Str: 12

| 谦虚 | qiānxū | modest, self-effacing, make modest remarks [5] |
| 谦逊 | qiānxùn | modest, humble, humility [6] |

浅 qiǎn
shallow

Rad: 氵   Str: 8

| 浅 | qiǎn | shallow, simple, superficial, light [5] |

qiàn
deficient, owe, to lack, yawn

Rad: 欠   Str: 4

欠   **qiàn**   owe, lack, yawn [5]

Additional words
哈欠 **hāqiàn** (yawn);
呵欠 **hēqiàn** (yawn).

枪

qiāng
gun, firearm, rifle, spear

Rad: 木   Str: 8

枪   **qiāng**   gun, spear [5]

Additional words
枪毙 **qiāngbì** (execute by shooting).

强

qiáng
strong, strength, force, power, powerful, better

qiǎng
strive

Rad: 弓   Str: 12

Notes
Also pronounced **jiàng** (stubborn, unbending).

坚强	**jiānqiáng**	strong, firm, tough [5]
强调	**qiángdiào**	to emphasise, stress [5]
强烈	**qiángliè**	intense, strong, violent [5]
倔强	**juéqiáng**	stubborn, unbending [6]
勉强	**miǎnqiǎng**	barely enough, reluctant, force sb. to do sth [6]
强制	**qiángzhì**	to enforce, enforcement, forcibly, compulsory [6]
强迫	**qiǎngpò**	to force, compel, coerce [6]
顽强	**wánqiáng**	tenacious, indomitable [6]

Additional words
强盗 **qiángdào** (robber).

qiáng
wall

Rad: 土   Str: 14

墙   **qiáng**   wall [5]

<u>Additional words</u>
墙壁 **qiángbì** (wall); 一堵墙 **yì dǔ qiáng** (a wall).

qiǎng
fight over, to rush, to scramble, to grab, to rob, to snatch

Rad: 扌   Str: 7

抢   **qiǎng**   snatch, grab, scramble, fight over [5]

抢劫   **qiǎngjié**   to rob [6]
抢救   **qiǎngjiù**   rescue, save [6]

qiāo
quiet, sad

Rad: 忄   Str: 10

悄悄   **qiāoqiāo**   quietly, secretly, stealthily [5]

qiáo
look at

Rad: 目   Str: 17

瞧   **qiáo**   look, see [5]

勤

qín
diligent, frequent

Rad: 力   Str: 13

勤奋	**qínfèn**	hardworking [5]
后勤	**hòuqín**	rear service, logistics [6]
勤俭	**qínjiǎn**	hardworking and thrifty [6]
勤劳	**qínláo**	hardworking, diligent, industrious, assiduous [6]
辛勤	**xīnqín**	industrious, hardworking [6]

青

qīng
blue-green

Rad: 青   Str: 8

青	**qīng**	green or blue, youth [5]
青春	**qīngchūn**	youth, youthfulness, youthful age [5]
青少年	**qīngshàonián**	juvenile, adolescent, teenager, teenage [5]

Additional words
青年 **qīngnián** (youth);
青铜 **qīngtóng** (bronze).

庆

qìng
celebrate

Rad: 广   Str: 6

| 国庆节 | **guóqìngjié** | National Day (October 1) [5] |
| 庆祝 | **qìngzhù** | celebrate [5] |

Additional words
庆贺 **qìnghè** (celebrate);
庆幸 **qìngxìng** (rejoice).

趋

qū
to hasten, to hurry, walk fast

Rad: 走   Str: 12

| 趋势 | **qūshì** | trend, tendency [5] |

屈

qū

bent, feel wronged

Rad: 尸   Str: 8

| 委屈 | **wěiqu** | to feel wronged, to nurse a grievance, to cause sb to feel wronged [5] |
| 屈服 | **qūfú** | to surrender, to yield [6] |

娶

qǔ

take a wife

Rad: 女   Str: 11

| 娶 | **qǔ** | marry (a woman), take a wife [5] |

圈

quān

to confine, enclose, pen (pig), a fold, circle, ring, loop

Rad: 囗   Str: 11

| 圈 | **quān** | to confine, enclose, a fold, circle, ring, loop, measure word (for loops, orbits, laps of a race) [5] |
| 圈套 | **quāntào** | trap, snare [6] |

权

quán

right, power, authority

Rad: 木   Str: 6

权力	**quánlì**	power, authority, jurisdiction [5]
权利	**quánlì**	power, right, privilege [5]
权衡	**quánhéng**	to weigh, balance, weigh up [6]
权威	**quánwēi**	authority [6]
政权	**zhèngquán**	political power, regime [6]
主权	**zhǔquán**	sovereign rights, sovereignty [6]

quán
fist

Rad: 手   Str: 10

| 太极拳 | **tàijíquán** | Taiji (shadow boxing) [5] |
| 拳头 | **quántou** | fist [6] |

quàn
to advise, to urge, to try to persuade, exhort

Rad: 力   Str: 4

| 劝 | **quàn** | persuade [5] |

qún
crowd, flock, group

Rad: 羊   Str: 13

| 群 | **qún** | group, crowd, flock, herd etc [5] |
| 群众 | **qúnzhòng** | multitude, the masses [6] |

rán
burn, combustion

Rad: 火   Str: 16

| 燃烧 | **ránshāo** | burn, kindle [5] |

Additional words
燃料 **ránliào** (fuel).

rào
go around, to wind (around)

Rad: 纟   Str: 9

绕	**rào**	go around, wind, coil (thread) [5]
围绕	**wéirào**	round, surround, revolve around [5]
缠绕	**chánrào**	to twist, twine, wind, pester, bother [6]

rěn
to beat, to endure, to tolerate

Rad: 心   Str: 7

忍不住	**rěnbuzhù**	cannot help, cannot resist, cannot bear [5]
残忍	**cánrěn**	brutal, cruel [6]
忍耐	**rěnnài**	restrain oneself, repress (anger etc.), exercise patience [6]
忍受	**rěnshòu**	to bear, endure, tolerate, put up with (pain, hardship etc.) [6]
容忍	**róngrěn**	to put up with, tolerate [6]

róng
glory, honored

Rad: 艹   Str: 9

繁荣	**fánróng**	flourishing, prosperous, prosperity [5]
光荣	**guāngróng**	glory, honour [6]
荣幸	**róngxìng**	honoured [6]
荣誉	**róngyù**	honour, glory [6]
欣欣向荣	**xīnxīn xiàngróng**	flourishing, prosperous [6]
虚荣	**xūróng**	vanity [6]

róu
soft

Rad: 木   Str: 9

| 温柔 | **wēnróu** | soft, mild, gentle [5] |
| 柔和 | **róuhé** | soft, mild [6] |

Additional words
柔软 **róuruǎn** (soft).

ruǎn
soft, flexible

Rad: 车   Str: 8

| 软 | **ruǎn** | soft [5] |
| 软件 | **ruǎnjiàn** | software (computer) [5] |

Additional words
柔软 **róuruǎn** (soft).

rùn
smooth, moist

Rad: 氵   Str: 10

利润	**lìrùn**	profit [5]
湿润	**shīrùn**	moist, damp, humid [5]
滋润	**zīrùn**	moisten [6]

弱

ruò
weak, feeble, young, inferior

Rad: 弓   Str: 10

弱	**ruò**	weak [5]
薄弱	**bóruò**	weak, frail [6]
脆弱	**cuìruò**	flimsy, frail [6]
弱点	**ruòdiǎn**	weakness [6]
削弱	**xuēruò**	weaken, cripple [6]

Additional words
微弱 **wēiruò** (faint).

洒

sǎ
spill, sprinkle

Rad: 氵   Str: 9

| 洒 | **sǎ** | sprinkle [5] |
| 潇洒 | **xiāosǎ** | natural and unrestrained [6] |

99

sǎng

throat, voice

Rad: 口   Str: 13

| 嗓子 | **sǎngzi** | throat, larynx, voice [5] |

shā

to kill, to murder, to slaughter

Rad: 木   Str: 6

| 杀 | **shā** | to kill, murder [5] |
| 抹杀 | **mǒshā** | to erase, obliterate evidence [6] |

Additional words
绞杀 **jiǎoshā** (strangle).

shǎ

foolish

Rad: 亻   Str: 13

| 傻 | **shǎ** | foolish [5] |

Additional words
傻子 **shǎzi** (idiot).

shà

tall building

Rad: 厂   Str: 12

Notes
Also pronounced **xià** (Xiamen city (Amoy)).

| 大厦 | **dàshà** | mansion, large building [5] |

shài

to sun

Rad: 日   Str: 10

| 晒 | **shài** | shine on, dry in the sun, sunbathe [5] |

shān

to delete

Rad: 刂   Str: 7

| 删除 | **shānchú** | to delete [5] |

shǎn

flash, lightning

Rad: 门   Str: 5

| 闪电 | **shǎndiàn** | lightning [5] |
| 闪烁 | **shǎnshuò** | twinkle, glimmer, flicker [6] |

shàn

to fan, measure word (for doors, windows, etc.)

Rad: 户   Str: 10

| 扇子 | **shànzi** | fan (that can create airflow through waving) [5] |

shàn
good

Rad: 口   Str: 12

改善	gǎishàn	to make better, to improve [5]
善良	shànliáng	kind, virtuous [5]
善于	shànyú	be good at, be adept in [5]
完善	wánshàn	perfect, to make perfect, to improve [5]
慈善	císhàn	charity, philanthropy [6]
妥善	tuǒshàn	proper, appropriate [6]

shǎng
enjoy the beauty of, give

Rad: 贝   Str: 12

| 欣赏 | xīnshǎng | appreciate, enjoy, admire, like [5] |
| 奖赏 | jiǎngshǎng | reward, prize [6] |

shàng
still, yet, to value, to esteem

Rad: 小   Str: 8

时尚	shíshàng	fashion, style, vogue [5]
高尚	gāoshàng	noble, lofty, sublime [6]
礼尚往来	lǐshàng wǎnglái	reciprocity, to pay back in kind, one good turn deserves another [6]
尚且	shàngqiě	even [6]

Additional words
和尚 **héshàng** (Buddhist monk).

shé
snake, serpent

Rad: 虫   Str: 11

| 蛇 | shé | snake [5] |
| 画蛇添足 | huàshé tiānzú | ruin by adding sth superfluous (lit. draw legs on a snake) [6] |

舍

shè
residence

Rad: 舌   Str: 8

舍不得	**shěbude**	hate to part with/spend/use, begrudge [5]
宿舍	**sùshè**	hostel, living quarters, dormitory [5]
锲而不舍	**qiè'ér bùshě**	work with perseverance [6]

射

shè
shoot, radio- (chem.)

Rad: 寸   Str: 10

射击	**shèjī**	to shoot, to fire (a gun) [5]
发射	**fāshè**	to shoot (a projectile), to fire (a rocket), to launch, to emit (a particle), to discharge, emanation, emission [6]
反射	**fǎnshè**	to reflect, reflection (from a mirror etc), reflex (i.e. automatic reaction of organism) [6]
放射	**fàngshè**	to radiate, radioactive [6]
辐射	**fúshè**	radiation [6]
注射	**zhùshè**	inject, shoot [6]

设

shè
to set up, to arrange, to establish, to found, to display

Rad: 讠   Str: 6

假设	**jiǎshè**	suppose that, hypothesis, conjecture [5]
建设	**jiànshè**	to build, construct, construction [5]
设备	**shèbèi**	equipment, facilities [5]
设计	**shèjì**	plan, design, to design, to plan [5]
设施	**shèshī**	facilities, installation, establishment [5]
设立	**shèlì**	to set up, establish [6]
设想	**shèxiǎng**	to imagine, have consideration for, idea, tentative plan [6]
设置	**shèzhì**	to set up, to install [6]
想方设法	**xiǎngfāng shèfǎ**	do everything possible, try every means [6]

shè
assist, collect, absorb

Rad: 扌   Str: 13

摄影	**shèyǐng**	to take a photo, shoot (a film) [5]
摄氏度	**shèshìdù**	degrees Celsius [6]

Additional words
拍摄 **pāishè** (take a picture).

shēn
to stretch, to extend

Rad: 亻   Str: 7

伸	**shēn**	stretch [5]
延伸	**yánshēn**	extend, stretch [6]

Additional words
伸懒腰 **shēn lǎnyāo** (stretch oneself).

shén
spirit, soul, God, unusual, mysterious, lively, spiritual being

Rad: 礻   Str: 9

精神	**jīngshén**	spirit, mind, consciousness, essence [5]
神话	**shénhuà**	mythology, myth, fairy tale [5]
神秘	**shénmì**	mysterious, mystical [5]
出神	**chūshén**	entranced [6]
聚精会神	**jùjīnghuìshén**	with complete concentration, with rapt attention [6]
留神	**liúshén**	to take care, to be careful [6]
神经	**shénjīng**	nerve [6]
神奇	**shénqí**	miraculous, magical [6]
神气	**shénqì**	expression, manner, spirited, vigorous, proud, cocky [6]
神圣	**shénshèng**	sacred, holy [6]
神态	**shéntài**	appearance, manner, bearing, look, expression [6]
神仙	**shénxiān**	supernatural being, immortal, fairy [6]
眼神	**yǎnshén**	expression in one's eyes [6]

慎 **shèn**
cautious

Rad: 忄   Str: 13

| 谨慎 | **jǐnshèn** | cautious, prudent, circumspect, careful, mindful [5] |
| 慎重 | **shènzhòng** | careful, cautious, prudent, discreet [6] |

升 **shēng**
to raise, to hoist, to promote, ascend, peaceful, promoted

Rad: 十   Str: 4

| 升 | **shēng** | to raise, promote, metric litre [5] |
| 晋升 | **jìnshēng** | promote [6] |

绳 **shéng**
rope

Rad: 纟   Str: 11

| 绳子 | **shéngzi** | string, rope [5] |

胜 **shèng**
victorious, able to do, competent enough to

Rad: 月   Str: 9

名胜古迹	**míngshèng gǔjì**	place of historical interest [5]
胜利	**shènglì**	victory, triumph [5]
胜负	**shèngfù**	victory or defeat, the outcome of a battle [6]
优胜劣汰	**yōushèng liètài**	survival of the fittest [6]

shī
poem, poetry,
verse

Rad: 讠 Str: 8

诗　　**shī**　poem [5]

Additional words
诗人 **shīrén** (poet).

狮

shī
lion

Rad: 犭 Str: 9

狮子　　**shīzi**　lion [5]

---

shī
moist, wet

Rad: 氵 Str: 12

潮湿　　**cháoshī**　wet, humid, damp,
　　　　　　　　　moist [5]
湿润　　**shīrùn**　moist, damp,
　　　　　　　　　humid [5]

施

shī
distribute (alms), to do, to
execute, to carry out

Rad: 方 Str: 9

措施　　**cuòshī**　measure, step (to be
　　　　　　　　　taken) [5]
设施　　**shèshī**　facilities, installation,
　　　　　　　　　establishment [5]

施加　　**shījiā**　to exert (effort or
　　　　　　　　　pressure) [6]
施展　　**shīzhǎn**　put to good use [6]
实施　　**shíshī**　to put into effect,
　　　　　　　　　implement, carry out,
　　　　　　　　　enforce, execute [6]

shí
rock, stone

Rad: 石   Str: 5

石头	**shítou**	stone [5]
化石	**huàshí**	fossil [6]
石油	**shíyóu**	petroleum [6]
岩石	**yánshí**	rock [6]
钻石	**zuànshí**	diamond [6]

Additional words
础石 **chǔshí** (plinth);
敦煌石窟 **Dūnhuáng Shíkū** (Gansu Caves).

shí
animal feed, eat, food, to feed

Rad: 食   Str: 9

粮食	**liángshi**	grain, food [5]
零食	**língshí**	snack [5]
食物	**shíwù**	food [5]
废寝忘食	**fèiqǐnwàngshí**	be so absorbed as to forget to eat and sleep [6]
素食	**sùshí**	vegetables, vegetarian food [6]
饮食	**yǐnshí**	food and drink [6]

Additional words
食堂 **shítáng** (dining hall, canteen).

shǐ
hasten, proceed to, sail a vessel

Rad: 马   Str: 8

驾驶	**jiàshǐ**	drive, pilot, steer, navigate [5]

shì
adorn, ornaments

Rad: 饣   Str: 8

装饰	**zhuāngshì**	decorate, adorn, ornament, accessory [5]
首饰	**shǒushì**	jewellery [6]
掩饰	**yǎnshì**	cover up, conceal [6]

shì
conditions, influence, tendency

Rad: 力   Str: 8

shǒu
to guard

Rad: 宀   Str: 6

趋势	qūshì	trend, tendency [5]
形势	xíngshì	situation, circumstances [5]
优势	yōushì	superiority, dominance, advantage [5]
姿势	zīshì	posture, gesture, pose, carriage [5]
地势	dìshì	terrain, topography in terms of strategic significance [6]
局势	júshì	situation [6]
气势	qìshì	vigour, look of great force or imposing manner [6]
声势	shēngshì	impetus, momentum [6]
势必	shìbì	certainly will, is bound to happen [6]
势力	shìlì	force (political, economic or military), power, influence [6]
手势	shǒushì	gesture, sign, signal [6]

遵守	zūnshǒu	to comply with, abide by, respect (an agreement) [5]
保守	bǎoshǒu	to guard, keep, conservative [6]
防守	fángshǒu	defend, guard (against) [6]
守护	shǒuhù	to guard, protect, guardianship [6]

Additional words
守株待兔 **shǒuzhūdàitù** (trust to chance and luck in one's actions, hope for gains without pains (lit. guarding a tree trunk to wait for a rabbit)).

shòu
long life

Rad: 寸   Str: 7

寿命	shòumìng	life span, life expectancy [5]

梳

shū
comb

Rad: 木   Str: 11

梳子   **shūzi**   comb [5]

蔬

shū
vegetables

Rad: 艹   Str: 15

蔬菜   **shūcài**   vegetable, greens [5]

殊

shū
unique

Rad: 歹   Str: 10

特殊   **tèshū**   special, peculiar, exceptional [5]

悬殊   **xuánshū**   wide gap, disparity [6]

属

shǔ
belong to, be subordinate to, genus (taxonomy), be born in the year of (one of the 12 animals), family members

Rad: 尸   Str: 12

金属   **jīnshǔ**   metal [5]
属于   **shǔyú**   belong to, be a part of [5]
附属   **fùshǔ**   subordinate, pertain to [6]
家属   **jiāshǔ**   family member, family dependent [6]
下属   **xiàshǔ**   subordinate, underling [6]

shǔ
rat, mouse

Rad: 鼠   Str: 13

| 老鼠 | **lǎoshǔ** | rat, mouse [5] |
| 鼠标 | **shǔbiāo** | mouse (computing) [5] |

Additional words
鼠年 **shǔnián** (year of Rat (1st year));
松鼠 **sōngshǔ** (squirrel).

shù
to state, to tell, to narrate, to relate

Rad: 辶   Str: 8

叙述	**xùshù**	narrate, relate, recount [5]
阐述	**chǎnshù**	to expound, elaborate (on a topic) [6]
陈述	**chénshù**	to declare, state, mention [6]

Additional words
描述 **miáoshù** (describe).

shuāi
throw on ground, to fall

Rad: 扌   Str: 14

| 摔倒 | **shuāidǎo** | trip, fall, stumble [5] |

Additional words
摔交 **shuāijiāo** (wrestling).

shuǎi
fling

Rad: 用   Str: 5

| 甩 | **shuǎi** | fling, throw [5] |

税 shuì
taxes, duties

Rad: 禾   Str: 12

| 税 | **shuì** | tax, duty, tariff [5] |

丝 sī
silk, thread, trace

Rad: 一   Str: 5

丝绸	**sīchóu**	silk [5]
丝毫	**sīháo**	very little, of the slightest amount or degree [5]
一丝不苟	**yìsībùgǒu**	meticulous, meticulously [6]

私 sī
personal, private, selfish

Rad: 禾   Str: 7

私人	**sīrén**	private, personal [5]
自私	**zìsī**	selfish, self-centred, self-concerned [5]
私自	**sīzì**	private, personal, secretly, without explicit approval [6]
隐私	**yǐnsī**	secrets [6]
走私	**zǒusī**	to smuggle [6]

撕 sī
to tear

Rad: 扌   Str: 15

| 撕 | **sī** | tear up [5] |

Additional words
撕毁 **sīhuǐ** (tear apart).

111

似

sì
to seem, to appear, similar, like, to resemble

shì
alike

Rad: 亻   Str: 6

似的	**shìde**	seem as if [5]
似乎	**sìhū**	it seems, as if, seemingly [5]
相似	**xiāngsì**	similar, alike [5]
类似	**lèisì**	similar, analogous [6]

搜

sōu
to search

Rad: 扌   Str: 12

搜索	**sōusuǒ**	to search, look for sth, look sth up, internet search [5]

Additional words
搜集 **sōují** (collect).

俗

sú
vulgar, popular

Rad: 亻   Str: 9

风俗	**fēngsú**	social custom [5]
俗话	**súhuà**	popular saying, folk adage, proverb [6]
通俗	**tōngsú**	common, everyday, average [6]
习俗	**xísú**	custom, tradition [6]
庸俗	**yōngsú**	tacky, filthy, vulgar [6]

宿

sù
lodge for the night, old, former, (a) night

Rad: 宀   Str: 11

宿舍	**sùshè**	hostel, living quarters, dormitory [5]

sù
respectful

Rad: 聿   Str: 8

严肃   **yánsù**   serious, solemn [5]

Additional words
肃清 **sùqīng** (eliminate).

sù
plain, element

Rad: 糸   Str: 10

因素	**yīnsù**	factor, element [5]
朴素	**pǔsù**	simple, plain [6]
素食	**sùshí**	vegetables, vegetarian food [6]
素质	**sùzhì**	inner quality, basic essence, change over time [6]
维生素	**wéishēngsù**	vitamin [6]
要素	**yàosù**	factor, element [6]
元素	**yuánsù**	element, element of a set, chemical element [6]

suì
to break down, to break into pieces, fragmentary

Rad: 石   Str: 13

碎	**suì**	to break down, broken, fragmentary [5]
粉碎	**fěnsuì**	break into pieces, grind, smash, shatter, crush [6]

sǔn
to damage, injure, to lose, to harm

Rad: 扌   Str: 10

损失	**sǔnshī**	to lose, damage, loss [5]
亏损	**kuīsǔn**	deficit, financial loss [6]
损坏	**sǔnhuài**	damage, break, spoil [6]

suō

to withdraw, to pull back, to contract, to shrink, to reduce

Rad: 纟 Str: 14

缩短	**suōduǎn**	shorten, curtail, cut short [5]
收缩	**shōusuō**	to pull back, to shrink, to contract [6]
压缩	**yāsuō**	suppress, stifle, inhibit, keep down [6]

suǒ

to lock

Rad: 钅 Str: 12

锁	**suǒ**	to lock up, to lock [5]
封锁	**fēngsuǒ**	blockade, seal off, cut off from the outside world [6]
连锁	**liánsuǒ**	chain [6]

suǒ

to search, to demand

Rad: 糸 Str: 10

搜索	**sōusuǒ**	to search, look for sth, look sth up, internet search [5]
摸索	**mōsuǒ**	to feel about, grope, fumble, do things slowly [6]
思索	**sīsuǒ**	to think deeply, ponder [6]
索取	**suǒqǔ**	to ask, demand [6]
索性	**suǒxìng**	you might as well (do it), simply, just [6]
探索	**tànsuǒ**	try to find (information), explore, probe [6]
线索	**xiànsuǒ**	trail, clues, thread (of a story) [6]

tān

beach, shoal

Rad: 氵 Str: 13

| 沙滩 | **shātān** | sand bar, beach [5] |

 **tǎn**
flat, open-hearted, level, smooth

Rad: 土   Str: 8

坦率	**tǎnshuài**	open, frank, candid [5]
平坦	**píngtǎn**	level, even, smooth, flat [6]
坦白	**tǎnbái**	honest, forthcoming, to confess [6]

Additional words
坦然 **tǎnrán** (calm).

 **tǎn**
blanket, rug

Rad: 毛   Str: 12

地毯	**dìtǎn**	carpet, rug [5]

炭 **tàn**
carbon, charcoal

Rad: 火   Str: 9

煤炭	**méitàn**	coal [5]

塘 **táng**
pond

Rad: 土   Str: 13

池塘	**chítáng**	pool, pond [5]

tàng
to scald, to burn, to iron, hot

Rad: 火　Str: 10

烫　　**tàng**　scald, burn, iron, perm [5]

táo
to escape, to run away, to flee

Rad: 辶　Str: 9

逃　　**táo**　to escape, flee [5]
逃避　**táobì**　evade, shirk [5]

Additional words
逃跑 **táopǎo** (escape, flee, run away).

táo
peach

Rad: 木　Str: 10

桃　　**táo**　peach [5]

Additional words
核桃 **hétao** (walnut).

táo
cleanse, eliminate, to clean out, to wash

Rad: 氵　Str: 11

淘气　**táoqì**　naughty [5]
淘汰　**táotài**　be sifted out, natural selection [6]

tào

to cover, covering, case, cover, sheath, measure word (for sets, collections)

Rad: 大   Str: 10

手套	**shǒutào**	glove [5]
套	**tào**	cover with, encase, measure word (for sets, collections) [5]
配套	**pèitào**	form a complete set [6]
圈套	**quāntào**	trap, snare [6]

tì

to substitute for, to take the place of, to replace, for, on behalf of, to stand in for

Rad: 曰   Str: 12

| 代替 | **dàitì** | instead, to replace, to substitute [5] |

tì

drawer, tier, tray

Rad: 尸   Str: 8

| 抽屉 | **chōuti** | drawer [5] |

tì

sneeze

Rad: 口   Str: 17

| 打喷嚏 | **dǎpēntì** | to sneeze [5] |

tiāo
choose, incite, carry on a pole

tiǎo
povoke

Rad: 扌   Str: 9

挑战	**tiǎozhàn**	challenge [5]
挑剔	**tiāoti**	picky, fussy [6]
挑拨	**tiǎobō**	provoke [6]
挑衅	**tiǎoxìn**	provoke, defy, defiance [6]

tiē
to stick, to paste, to keep close to, to fit snugly, subsidize, allowance

Rad: 贝   Str: 9

体贴	**tǐtiē**	show consideration for [5]
粘贴	**zhāntiē**	to plaster, stick, paste [5]
补贴	**bǔtiē**	to subsidise, subsidy, allowance [6]

Additional words
锅贴 **guōtiē** (fried dumpling).

tíng
court, courtyard

Rad: 广   Str: 9

家庭	**jiātíng**	family, household [5]

Additional words
法庭 **fǎtíng** (court).

tǒng
to gather, unite, unify, whole, order, system

Rad: 纟   Str: 9

传统	**chuántǒng**	tradition, traditional, convention, conventional [5]
统一	**tǒngyī**	unify, unite, unified [5]
系统	**xìtǒng**	system [5]
总统	**zǒngtǒng**	president (of a country) [5]
统筹兼顾	**tǒngchóu jiāngù**	overall plan taking all factors into account [6]
统计	**tǒngjì**	statistics, to count, to add up [6]
统统	**tǒngtǒng**	totally, wholly [6]
统治	**tǒngzhì**	to rule, dominate [6]

tòng
ache, pain, sorrow

Rad: 疒   Str: 12

| 痛苦 | tòngkǔ | painful, suffering [5] |
| 痛快 | tòngkuài | very happy, delighted [5] |

tōu
to steal

Rad: 亻   Str: 11

| 偷 | tōu | steal [5] |

tóu
to throw, to send

Rad: 扌   Str: 7

投入	tóurù	put into, throw into, invest, investment [5]
投资	tóuzī	investment, to invest [5]
投机	tóujī	to speculate (on financial markets), opportunistic, congenial, agreeable [6]
投票	tóupiào	vote, poll [6]
投诉	tóusù	lodge a complaint [6]
投降	tóuxiáng	surrender, capitulate, give up resistance [6]
投掷	tóuzhì	throw, toss [6]

tòu
to penetrate, thorough, penetrating, to pass through, to pierce

Rad: 辶   Str: 10

透明	tòumíng	transparent, lucid [5]
渗透	shèntòu	infiltrate, pervade, osmosis [6]
透露	tòulù	divulge, reveal [6]

Additional words
透镜 tòujìng (lens).

Sheldon Smith

途 **tú**
way, route, road

Rad: 辶　Str: 10

长途	**chángtú**	long distance [5]
前途	**qiántú**	prospects, future outlook [5]
用途	**yòngtú**	use, purpose, application [5]
半途而废	**bàntúérfèi**	give up halfway, leave sth unfinished [6]
途径	**tújìng**	way, approach, avenue, channel [6]

涂 **tú**
to smear, daub, to apply (paint), to spread

Rad: 氵　Str: 10

糊涂	**hútu**	muddled, confused, bewildered [5]
涂抹	**túmǒ**	to paint, smear, daub [6]

Additional words

涂料 **túliào** (coating).

土 **tǔ**
earth, dust

Rad: 土　Str: 3

土地	**tǔdì**	land, soil, territory [5]
土豆	**tǔdòu**	potato [5]
风土人情	**fēngtǔ rénqíng**	local customs [6]
领土	**lǐngtǔ**	territory [6]
土壤	**tǔrǎng**	soil [6]

Additional words

泥土 **nítǔ** (soil).

吐 **tù**
vomit

Rad: 口　Str: 6

吐	**tù**	to vomit, throw up [5]
呕吐	**ǒutù**	to vomit, throw up [6]
吞吞吐吐	**tūntūn tǔtǔ**	hem and haw, procrastinate [6]

tù
rabbit

Rad: 刀   Str: 8

兔子   **tùzi**   hare, rabbit [5]

Additional words
守株待兔 **shǒuzhūdàitù** (trust to chance and luck in one's actions, hope for gains without pains (lit. guarding a tree trunk to wait for a rabbit)).

tuán
regiment, round, circular, group, society

Rad: 囗   Str: 6

团	**tuán**	regiment, round, circular, group, society [5]
集团	**jítuán**	group, bloc [6]
团结	**tuánjié**	a rally, to hold a rally, to join forces [6]
团体	**tuántǐ**	group, organisation, team [6]
团圆	**tuányuán**	reunion [6]

tuì
retreat, to decline, to move back, to withdraw

Rad: 辶   Str: 9

退	**tuì**	return, give back, withdraw, fade [5]
退步	**tuìbù**	to regress, fall behind, retrogression [5]
退休	**tuìxiū**	retire (from work) [5]
撤退	**chètuì**	to withdraw, retreat [6]
衰退	**shuāituì**	to decline, fall, drop, recession (in economics) [6]

tuō
to hold in one's hand, to entrust

Rad: 扌   Str: 6

摩托车	**mótuōchē**	motorcycle, motorbike [5]
拜托	**bàituō**	to request (sb to do sth) [6]
衬托	**chèntuō**	to set off, relieve [6]
寄托	**jìtuō**	to have sb look after sb, to place (hope etc.) on [6]
托运	**tuōyùn**	to consign (goods), to check (baggage) [6]
委托	**wěituō**	consign, commission, delegate, devolve [6]
依托	**yītuō**	rely on, depend on [6]

歪 wāi
askew

Rad: 止 Str: 9

| 歪 | wāi | askew, crooked, awry [5] |
| 歪曲 | wāiqū | distort, misrepresent, twist, contort [6] |

弯 wān
bend, bent

Rad: 弓 Str: 9

| 拐弯 | guǎiwān | turn a corner, make a turn, change direction [5] |

王 wáng
king

Rad: 王 Str: 4

| 国王 | guówáng | king [5] |
| 王子 | wángzǐ | prince [5] |

Additional words
王国 **wángguó** (kingdom, realm, domain).

威 wēi
power, might, prestige

Rad: 女 Str: 9

威胁	wēixié	to threaten, menace [5]
权威	quánwēi	authority [6]
示威	shìwēi	to demonstrate (as a protest), a demonstration, a military show of force [6]
威风	wēifēng	power, impressive force [6]
威力	wēilì	might, power [6]
威望	wēiwàng	prestige [6]
威信	wēixìn	prestige, trust [6]

违 wéi
to disobey, to violate, to separate, to go against

Rad: 辶   Str: 7

| 违反 | wéifǎn | to violate (a law) [5] |
| 违背 | wéibèi | to violate, run counter to [6] |

Additional words
违法 wéifǎ (break the law).

唯 wéi
only, sole

Rad: 口   Str: 11

| 唯一 | wéiyī | only, sole [5] |
| 唯独 | wéidú | alone, only, unique [6] |

维 wéi
to preserve, to maintain, to hold together, dimension

Rad: 纟   Str: 11

维修	wéixiū	to mend, repair, maintenance [5]
思维	sīwéi	thinking, thought [6]
维持	wéichí	to keep, to maintain, to preserve [6]
维护	wéihù	to safeguard, defend [6]
维生素	wéishēngsù	vitamin [6]
纤维	xiānwéi	fibre [6]

伟 wěi
big, large, great

Rad: 亻   Str: 6

伟大	wěidà	great, mighty [5]
宏伟	hóngwěi	grand, imposing, magnificent [6]
雄伟	xióngwěi	grand, magnificent [6]

wěi
tail

Rad: 尸   Str: 7

尾巴   **wěiba**   tail [5]

<u>Additional words</u>
翘尾巴 **qiào wěiba** (to be cocky, be snobbish and self-important (lit. to hold up the tail)).

wěi
crooked, give up, indeed, to commission

Rad: 女   Str: 8

委屈   **wěiqu**   to feel wronged, to nurse a grievance, to cause sb to feel wronged [5]

委托   **wěituō**   consign, commission, delegate, devolve [6]

委员   **wěiyuán**   committee member [6]

<u>Additional words</u>
委员会 **wěiyuánhuì** (committee).

wèi
not yet, did not, have not, not, 1-3 p.m., 8th earthly branch

Rad: 木   Str: 5

未必   **wèibì**   not necessarily, may not, perhaps not [5]

未来   **wèilái**   future [5]

未免   **wèimiǎn**   a bit too much, over the top (you exaggerate) [6]

wèi
stomach

Rad: 月   Str: 9

胃   **wèi**   stomach [5]
胃口   **wèikǒu**   appetite [5]

慰

wèi
reassure

Rad: 心 Str: 15

安慰	**ānwèi**	to comfort, to console, consolation [5]
慰问	**wèiwèn**	express sympathy for [6]
欣慰	**xīnwèi**	glad, gratified [6]

谓

wèi
speak of

Rad: 讠 Str: 11

无所谓	**wúsuǒwèi**	be indifferent, not care, cannot be called [5]

Additional words
所谓 **suǒwèi** (so-called).

吻

wěn
kiss, mouth

Rad: 口 Str: 7

吻	**wěn**	lips, kiss, touch or caress with one's lips [5]

稳

wěn
settled, steady, stable

Rad: 禾 Str: 14

稳定	**wěndìng**	stable, steady [5]

Additional words
稳当 **wěndang** (reliable).

wò
to lie, to crouch

Rad: 卜   Str: 8

| 卧室 | **wòshì** | bedroom [5] |

wò
shake hands, to hold, to grasp

Rad: 扌   Str: 12

把握	**bǎwò**	to grasp, seize, hold, assurance, certainty, sure (of the outcome) [5]
握手	**wòshǒu**	to shake hands [5]
掌握	**zhǎngwò**	to grasp, master, know well, to seize (initiative, opportunity, destiny) [5]

wū
room, house

Rad: 尸   Str: 9

| 屋子 | **wūzi** | room [5] |

Additional words
屋顶 **wūdǐng** (roof).

wǔ
martial, military

Rad: 止   Str: 8

武术	**wǔshù**	military skill or technique (in former times), martial arts (also called 功夫 gōngfu) [5]
武器	**wǔqì**	weapon, arms [6]
武侠	**wǔxiá**	martial arts [6]
武装	**wǔzhuāng**	weaponry, arm forces, arm, equip [6]

勿 wù
do not

Rad: 勹   Str: 4

勿   **wù**   not [5]

雾 wù
fog, mist

Rad: 雨   Str: 13

雾   **wù**   fog, mist [5]

Additional words
烟雾 **yānwù** (smoke, mist).

析 xī
to separate, to divide, to analyze

Rad: 木   Str: 8

分析   **fēnxī**   to analyse, analysis [5]

夕 xī
evening, dusk

Rad: 夕   Str: 3

除夕   **chúxī**   Chinese New Year's Eve [5]

夕阳   **xīyáng**   the setting sun [6]

127

xí
banquet, woven mat,
seat, place

Rad: 巾   Str: 10

出席	**chūxí**	attend, be present [5]
主席	**zhǔxí**	chairperson, premier, chairman [5]
缺席	**quēxí**	absence, absent [6]

xiā
blind

Rad: 目   Str: 15

| 瞎 | **xiā** | become blind, groundlessly, to no purpose, aimlessly [5] |

Additional words
瞎子 **xiāzi** (blind person).

xià
to frighten, to scare, to
intimidate, to
threaten

hè
threaten
Rad: 口   Str: 6

| 吓 | **xià** | to frighten, scare [5] |
| 恐吓 | **kǒnghè** | to threaten, menace [6] |

xián
to stay idle, to be
unoccupied, not busy,
leisure, enclosure

Rad: 门   Str: 7

空闲	**kòngxián**	leisure, idle time [5]
休闲	**xiūxián**	leisure [5]
闲话	**xiánhuà**	idle words, gossip, tattle, digression, complaint [6]

xiǎn
prominent, conspicuous

Rad: 日   Str: 9

明显	**míngxiǎn**	clear, obvious, apparent [5]
显得	**xiǎnde**	look, seem, appear [5]
显然	**xiǎnrán**	obvious, obviously [5]
显示	**xiǎnshì**	to show, to illustrate, to display, to demonstrate [5]
显著	**xiǎnzhù**	notable, marked, remarkable [6]

xiàn
a district, county

Rad: 厶   Str: 7

| 县 | **xiàn** | county [5] |

Additional words
县长 **xiànzhǎng** (county magistrate).

xiàn
limit, bound

Rad: 阝   Str: 8

限制	**xiànzhì**	to confine, restrict, limit, restriction [5]
极限	**jíxiàn**	limit, utmost [6]
界限	**jièxiàn**	boundary, limit, marginal [6]
局限	**júxiàn**	limit, confine [6]
期限	**qīxiàn**	time limit, deadline, allotted time [6]

Additional words
有限 **yǒuxiàn** (limited).

xiàn
to offer

Rad: 犬   Str: 13

贡献	**gòngxiàn**	contribute, dedicate, contribution [5]
奉献	**fèngxiàn**	dedicate, devote [6]
文献	**wénxiàn**	literature, document [6]

xiāng
side room

Rad: 厂　Str: 11

车厢	**chēxiāng**	railway carriage, railroad car [5]

xiāng
village, country

Rad: 乙　Str: 3

家乡	**jiāxiāng**	hometown, native place [5]
故乡	**gùxiāng**	hometown [6]
乡镇	**xiāngzhèn**	village, town [6]

xiǎng
enjoy

Rad: 亠　Str: 8

享受	**xiǎngshòu**	enjoy, enjoyment [5]

xiàng
back of neck, item, thing

Rad: 工　Str: 9

项	**xiàng**	item, thing, back of neck [5]
项链	**xiàngliàn**	necklace [5]
项目	**xiàngmù**	item, project [5]
事项	**shìxiàng**	matter, item [6]

 **xiāo**
to melt, to do away with, to sell

Rad: 钅 Str: 12

销售	xiāoshòu	sell [5]
报销	bàoxiāo	submit an expense account, apply for reimbursement [6]
畅销	chàngxiāo	sell well [6]
撤销	chèxiāo	repeal, retract [6]
推销	tuīxiāo	to market, sell [6]
销毁	xiāohuǐ	destroy (by melting or burning) [6]

Additional words
脱销 tuōxiāo (sold out).

 **xiào**
filial

Rad: 子 Str: 7

孝顺	xiàoshun	filial piety, be obedient to one's parents [5]

 **xiē**
to rest

Rad: 欠 Str: 13

歇	xiē	to rest [5]

Additional words
间歇 jiànxiē (intermission).

 **xié**
slanting

Rad: 斗 Str: 11

斜	xié	tilted, slanting [5]
倾斜	qīngxié	to incline, lean, slant, slope [6]

Additional words
斜边 xiébiān (hypotenuse).

肋 xié
threaten, side of body

Rad: 月　Str: 8

| 威胁 | **wēixié** | to threaten, menace [5] |

欣 xīn
happy

Rad: 欠　Str: 8

欣赏	**xīnshǎng**	appreciate, enjoy, admire, like [5]
欣慰	**xīnwèi**	glad, gratified [6]
欣欣向荣	**xīnxīn xiàngróng**	flourishing, prosperous [6]

形 xíng
to appear, look, form, shape

Rad: 彡　Str: 7

形成	**xíngchéng**	to take shape, form [5]
形容	**xíngróng**	to describe, description, appearance, look [5]
形势	**xíngshì**	situation, circumstances [5]
形式	**xíngshì**	form, shape, situation, circumstance [5]
形象	**xíngxiàng**	image, form, figure, visualization [5]
形状	**xíngzhuàng**	shape, figure, form [5]
情形	**qíngxīng**	circumstance, condition, situation [6]
形态	**xíngtài**	form, shape, pattern, morphology [6]

型 xíng
model

Rad: 土　Str: 9

大型	**dàxíng**	large-scale, large [5]
类型	**lèixíng**	type, category [5]
典型	**diǎnxíng**	typical case, model, typical, representative [6]
模型	**móxíng**	model, mould, matrix, pattern, die [6]
造型	**zàoxíng**	model, mould [6]

xiōng
elder brother

Rad: 儿　Str: 5

| 兄弟 | **xiōngdì** | older and younger brothers [5] |

xiōng
chest, bosom, heart, mind, thorax

Rad: 月　Str: 10

胸	**xiōng**	chest, bosom, heart, mind, thorax [5]
胸怀	**xiōnghuái**	mind, heart [6]
胸膛	**xiōngtáng**	chest, thorax [6]

xióng
heroic, male

Rad: 隹　Str: 12

英雄	**yīngxióng**	hero [5]
雌雄	**cíxióng**	male and female [6]
雄厚	**xiónghòu**	strong and solid, robust [6]
雄伟	**xióngwěi**	grand, magnificent [6]

xū
devoid of content, void, false, empty, vain

Rad: 虍　Str: 11

谦虚	**qiānxū**	modest, self-effacing, make modest remarks [5]
虚心	**xūxīn**	modest, open-minded [5]
空虚	**kōngxū**	hollow, emptiness [6]
虚假	**xūjiǎ**	false, phony, pretence [6]
虚荣	**xūróng**	vanity [6]
虚伪	**xūwěi**	false, hypocritical [6]

xù
narrate

Rad: 又   Str: 9

叙述   **xùshù**   narrate, relate, recount [5]

xù
beginnings, clues, mental state, thread

Rad: 纟   Str: 11

情绪   **qíngxù**   morale, feeling, mood [5]

<u>Additional words</u>
头绪 **tóuxù** (lead, clue).

xuān
to declare (publicly), to announce

Rad: 宀   Str: 9

宣布   **xuānbù**   to declare, announce [5]
宣传   **xuānchuán**   to publicise, propaganda [5]
宣誓   **xuānshì**   to swear an oath (of office) [6]
宣扬   **xuānyáng**   to proclaim, make public [6]

xuè
blood, blood

Rad: 血   Str: 6

<u>Notes</u>
Also pronounced **xiě** (blood).

血   **xuè**   blood (also pronounced xiě or xuě) [5]
心血   **xīnxuè**   heart's blood, meticulous care [6]
血压   **xuèyā**   blood pressure [6]

xún

to search, to look for, to seek

Rad: 寸   Str: 6

| 寻找 | **xúnzhǎo** | look for, seek [5] |
| 寻觅 | **xúnmì** | to seek, look for [6] |

询

xún

inquire

Rad: 讠   Str: 8

| 询问 | **xúnwèn** | ask about, inquire about, solicit opinions [5] |
| 咨询 | **zīxún** | refer, consult [5] |

xún

ten days, ten years

Rad: 日   Str: 6

| 中旬 | **zhōngxún** | period of the second ten days of a month [5] |

Additional words
上旬 **shàngxún** (first ten days of a month).

训

xùn

to train, to teach, instruction, example, pattern

Rad: 讠   Str: 5

教训	**jiàoxùn**	a lesson, a moral, to chide sb, to lecture sb [5]
培训	**péixùn**	to cultivate, train [5]
训练	**xùnliàn**	to train, drill, training [5]

xùn
rapid

Rad: 辶   Str: 6

迅速   **xùnsù**   rapid, speedy, quick [5]

押

yā
detain in custody

Rad: 扌   Str: 8

押金   **yājīn**   deposit, guarantee [5]

Additional words
押送 **yāsòng** (send under escort).

yán
to prolong, to extend, to delay

Rad: 廴   Str: 6

延长   **yáncháng**   to lengthen, prolong, extend [5]

蔓延	**mànyán**	extend, spread [6]
拖延	**tuōyán**	delay, put off [6]
延期	**yánqī**	to put off, delay, defer [6]
延伸	**yánshēn**	extend, stretch [6]
延续	**yánxù**	to continue, go on, last [6]

yàn
feast, repose

Rad: 宀   Str: 10

宴会   **yànhuì**   banquet, feast, dinner party [5]

艳

yàn
glamorous

Rad: 色   Str: 10

鲜艳   **xiānyàn**   brightly coloured [5]

痒

yǎng
to itch, to tickle

Rad: 疒   Str: 11

痒   **yǎng**   itchy [5]

腰

yāo
waist

Rad: 月   Str: 13

腰   **yāo**   waist [5]

Additional words
伸懒腰 **shēn lǎnyāo** (stretch oneself).

摇

yáo
shake, to rock

Rad: 扌   Str: 13

摇	**yáo**	sway, shake [5]
摇摆	**yáobǎi**	sway, swing, rock, wigwag, vacillate [6]
摇滚	**yáogǔn**	rock 'n' roll, rock [6]

Additional words
摇摆舞 **yáobǎiwǔ** (rock 'n' roll).

137

yǎo
bite, nip

Rad: 口   Str: 9

咬   **yǎo**   to bite, to nip [5]

yè
night

Rad: 夕   Str: 8

熬夜   **áoyè**   stay up late [5]
夜   **yè**   night, evening [5]
昼夜   **zhòuyè**   day and night [6]

Additional words
半夜 **bànyè** (midnight);
天方夜谭 **tiānfāngyètán** (the story of Arabian Nights).

yī
according to, depend on, near to

Rad: 亻   Str: 8

依然   **yīrán**   as before, still [5]
依旧   **yījiù**   as before, still like before [6]
依据   **yījù**   be in line with, base sth on, basis, grounds [6]
依靠   **yīkào**   rely on, depend on, backing, support [6]
依赖   **yīlài**   depend on, rely on [6]
依托   **yītuō**   rely on, depend on [6]

yí
to lose, to leave behind

Rad: 辶   Str: 12

遗憾   **yíhàn**   pity, regret [5]
遗产   **yíchǎn**   heritage, legacy, inheritance [6]
遗传   **yíchuán** heredity, inheritance, to transmit [6]
遗留   **yíliú**   leave behind, bequeath, hand down (to next generation) [6]
遗失   **yíshī**   to lose, lost [6]

yí
to move, to shift, to change, to alter, to remove

Rad: 禾　　Str: 11

移动	**yídòng**	mobile, movement, to move, shift [5]
移民	**yímín**	to immigrate, to migrate, emigrant, immigrant [5]
潜移默化	**qiányí mòhuà**	imperceptible influence, to influence secretly [6]
转移	**zhuǎnyí**	to shift, to divert or distract (attention etc) [6]

yì
a hundred million, calculate

Rad: 亻　　Str: 3

| 亿 | **yì** | a hundred million [5] |

yǐ
second in order, second heavenly stem, B (in a sequence involving "A", "B", "C", etc.)

Rad: 乙　　Str: 1

| 乙 | **yǐ** | the second of the ten Heavenly Stems, second (in order) [5] |

yì
justice, meaning

Rad: 丶　　Str: 3

义务	**yìwù**	duty, obligation, moral responsibility [5]
意义	**yìyì**	meaning, sense, significance [5]
贬义	**biǎnyì**	derogatory sense [6]
定义	**dìngyì**	definition [6]
含义	**hányì**	signification, meaning [6]
见义勇为	**jiànyì yǒngwéi**	never hesitate to do what is right (idiom from the Analects) [6]
正义	**zhèngyì**	righteousness, justice, just, righteous [6]
主义	**zhǔyì**	doctrine, -ism [6]

Additional words
侠义 **xiáyì** (chivalrous);
资本主义 **zīběnzhǔyì** (capitalism).

yì
descendents,
frontier

Rad: 衣   Str: 13

| 华裔 | **huáyì** | ethnic Chinese, non-Chinese citizen of Chinese ancestry [5] |

yì
benefit, increase

Rad: 皿   Str: 10

利益	**lìyì**	benefit, in sb's interest [5]
精益求精	**jīngyìqiújīng**	to perfect sth that is already outstanding, constantly improving [6]
日益	**rìyì**	more and more each day, increasingly [6]
收益	**shōuyì**	income, profit [6]
效益	**xiàoyì**	benefit [6]

yīn
marriage

Rad: 女   Str: 9

| 婚姻 | **hūnyīn** | marriage, wedding [5] |

yīng
brave

Rad: 艹   Str: 8

英俊	**yīngjùn**	handsome [5]
英雄	**yīngxióng**	hero [5]
英明	**yīngmíng**	brilliant, wise [6]
英勇	**yīngyǒng**	heroic, valiant, brave, gallant [6]

Additional words
英尺 **yīngchǐ** (foot (unit of measurement));
英国 **Yīngguó** (England).

yíng

to deal in, to trade, to operate, to run, camp, nourishment, to manage

Rad: 艹　Str: 11

经营	**jīngyíng**	manage, run, operate, plan and organise [5]
夏令营	**xiàlìngyíng**	summer camp [5]
营养	**yíngyǎng**	nutrition, nourishment [5]
营业	**yíngyè**	to do business, to trade [5]

Additional words
营火 **yínghuǒ** (campfire).

yìng

hard, stiff, strong, firm

Rad: 石　Str: 12

硬	**yìng**	hard, stiff, strong, firm [5]
硬件	**yìngjiàn**	hardware [5]
坚硬	**jiānyìng**	hard, stony, solid [6]
僵硬	**jiāngyìng**	stark, stiff [6]

Additional words
硬币 **yìngbì** (coin).

yìng

reflect, shine

Rad: 日　Str: 9

| 反映 | **fǎnyìng** | to mirror, reflect, mirror image, reflection, to report, make known [5] |

yōng

gather round, rush in, crowd, throng, to hold, crowded, to support

Rad: 扌　Str: 8

拥抱	**yōngbào**	embrace, hug [5]
拥挤	**yōngjǐ**	push, squeeze, press, shove [5]
拥护	**yōnghù**	support, uphold [6]
拥有	**yōngyǒu**	hold, possess of [6]

yōu
at ease, long (in time), sad

Rad: 心   Str: 11

悠久	**yōujiǔ**	long, age-old, longstanding [5]

yóu
as if, still, to scheme

Rad: 犭   Str: 7

犹豫	**yóuyù**	be unsure, hesitate [5]
犹如	**yóurú**	just as, like [6]

yòu
young

Rad: 幺   Str: 5

幼儿园	**yòu'éryuán**	kindergarten, nursery school [5]
幼稚	**yòuzhì**	childish, puerile, immature, naive [6]

yú
amuse

Rad: 女   Str: 10

娱乐	**yúlè**	to entertain, amuse, entertainment, hobby [5]

余

yú
extra, surplus, remaining

Rad: 人　Str: 7

多余	**duōyú**	unnecessary, needless, uncalled for, surplus [5]
其余	**qíyú**	the others, the rest, the remainder [5]
业余	**yèyú**	amateur, not professional [5]

屿

yǔ
islet

Rad: 山　Str: 6

岛屿	**dǎoyǔ**	islands and islets [5]

玉

yù
jade

Rad: 玉　Str: 5

玉米	**yùmǐ**	maize, corn [5]
玉	**yù**	jade [6]

豫

yù
beforehand, prepare

Rad: 豕　Str: 15

犹豫	**yóuyù**	be unsure, hesitate [5]

yù
reside, residence

Rad: 宀　Str: 12

| 公寓 | **gōngyù** | apartment building, block of flats [5] |
| 寓言 | **yùyán** | fable, allegory, parable [6] |

Additional words
寓所 **yùsuǒ** (residence).

yù
field, region, area, domain (taxonomy)

Rad: 土　Str: 11

| 领域 | **lǐngyù** | field, sphere, domain, realm, area, territory [5] |
| 区域 | **qūyù** | region, area, district [6] |

yuán
circle, round, circular, spherical, (of the moon) full, unit of Chinese currency (Yuan), tactful, to justify

Rad: 囗　Str: 10

圆	**yuán**	round, circular, circle [5]
方圆	**fāngyuán**	circumference [6]
团圆	**tuányuán**	reunion [6]
椭圆	**tuǒyuán**	ellipse [6]
圆满	**yuánmǎn**	perfect, satisfactory [6]

yuán
root, source, origin

Rad: 氵　Str: 13

能源	**néngyuán**	energy, power source [5]
资源	**zīyuán**	natural resource (e.g. water or minerals), resource (e.g. manpower or tourism) [5]
电源	**diànyuán**	power supply [6]
根源	**gēnyuán**	origin, root, source [6]
来源	**láiyuán**	source, origin [6]
起源	**qǐyuán**	origin, genesis, to originate, stem, start [6]
源泉	**yuánquán**	headspring, source [6]

yuàn
blame, complain

Rad: 心   Str: 9

抱怨	**bàoyuàn**	complain [5]
恩怨	**ēnyuàn**	feeling of resentment, grudge [6]
埋怨	**mányuàn**	complain [6]

yuè
to jump, to leap

Rad: 足   Str: 11

活跃	**huóyuè**	active, vigorous [5]
飞跃	**fēiyuè**	to leap [6]
跳跃	**tiàoyuè**	to jump, skip, leap [6]
踊跃	**yǒngyuè**	vying with one another, enthusiastic, eager [6]

yūn
confused, dizzy, faint, swoon, pass out

Rad: 日   Str: 10

晕	**yūn**	swoon, faint, pass out, lose consciousness [5]

Additional words
头晕 **tóuyūn** (dizzy).

yún
even, evenly (divided), uniform

Rad: 勹   Str: 4

均匀	**jūnyún**	even, uniform, well-distributed [5]

yùn
pregnant

Rad: 子 Str: 5

| 怀孕 | **huáiyùn** | become pregnant [5] |
| 孕育 | **yùnyù** | to be pregnant, produce offspring, nurture [6] |

Additional words
受孕 **shòuyùn** (conceive).

zāi
disaster, calamity

Rad: 火 Str: 7

| 灾害 | **zāihài** | calamity, disaster [5] |
| 灾难 | **zāinàn** | calamity, disaster, suffering [6] |

zài
to carry, to convey, to load, to hold

Rad: 车 Str: 10

| 下载 | **xiàzài** | to download (also pronounced xiàzài) [5] |
| 记载 | **jìzǎi** | record, put down in writing, chronicle [6] |

zàn
to praise, to patronize, to support

Rad: 贝 Str: 16

称赞	**chēngzàn**	praise, acclaim, commend [5]
赞成	**zànchéng**	agree with, approve of, favour [5]
赞美	**zànměi**	to admire, applause, praise, eulogize [5]
赞叹	**zàntàn**	highly praise [6]
赞助	**zànzhù**	support, sponsor [6]

糟 **zāo**
dregs, to waste, spoil

Rad: 米   Str: 17

| 糟糕 | **zāogāo** | too bad, how terrible, what bad luck, terrible, bad [5] |
| 糟蹋 | **zāotà** | waste, ruin, spoil [6] |

Additional words
糟踏 **zāota** (ruin, waste, insult, affront).

造 **zào**
to make, to build, to invent, to manufacture

Rad: 辶   Str: 10

创造	**chuàngzào**	to create, to bring about, to produce [5]
造成	**zàochéng**	bring about, cause, create [5]
制造	**zhìzào**	to manufacture, to make [5]
塑造	**sùzào**	to model, to mould, to portray (in sculpture or in words) [6]
伪造	**wěizào**	to forge, to fake, to counterfeit [6]
造型	**zàoxíng**	model, mould [6]
铸造	**zhùzào**	to cast (pour metal into a mould) [6]

皂 **zào**
soap

Rad: 白   Str: 7

| 肥皂 | **féizào** | soap [5] |

燥 **zào**
dry, parched, impatient

Rad: 火   Str: 17

| 干燥 | **gānzào** | to dry (of weather, paint, cement etc), desiccation, dull, uninteresting, arid [5] |
| 枯燥 | **kūzào** | dry and dull, uninteresting [6] |

炸

zhá
deep fry

zhà
explode

Rad: 火   Str: 9

油炸	**yóuzhá**	deep-fry, deep-fried [5]
爆炸	**bàozhà**	explode, blow up [6]

摘

zhāi
to borrow, to pick (flowers, fruit), to pluck, to take, to select

Rad: 扌   Str: 14

摘	**zhāi**	to pick (flowers, fruit), to pluck [5]
摘要	**zhāiyào**	summary, brief [6]

窄

zhǎi
narrow

Rad: 穴   Str: 10

窄	**zhǎi**	narrow, petty-minded [5]
狭窄	**xiázhǎi**	narrow [6]

粘

zhān
sticky, to stick, paste

Rad: 米   Str: 11

Notes
Also pronounced **nián** (sticky).

粘贴	**zhāntiē**	to plaster, stick, paste [5]

Additional words
粘糕 **niángāo** (sticky cake).

zhàn
fight, war, battle

Rad: 戈　Str: 9

挑战	**tiǎozhàn**	challenge [5]
战争	**zhànzhēng**	war, conflict [5]
战斗	**zhàndòu**	to fight, to battle [6]
战略	**zhànluè**	strategy [6]
战术	**zhànshù**	tactics (military), manoeuvre [6]
战役	**zhànyì**	military campaign [6]

zhǎng
to rise (of prices, rivers), to swell, distend

Rad: 氵　Str: 10

| 涨 | **zhǎng** | go up, rise (of prices, rivers) [5] |
| 高涨 | **gāozhǎng** | upsurge, run high (of tensions etc.) [6] |

zhǎng
in charge of, palm of hand

Rad: 手　Str: 12

| 鼓掌 | **gǔzhǎng** | to applaud [5] |
| 掌握 | **zhǎngwò** | to grasp, master, know well, to seize (initiative, opportunity, destiny) [5] |

zhàng
account

Rad: 贝　Str: 8

| 结账 | **jiézhàng** | to settle an account [5] |
| 账户 | **zhànghù** | bank account [5] |

zhào
to call together, to summon, to convene

Rad: 口   Str: 5

| 召开 | **zhàokāi** | to convene (a conference or meeting), to convoke, to call together [5] |
| 号召 | **hàozhào** | summon, call up, appeal, call [6] |

zhé
philosophy, wise

Rad: 口   Str: 10

| 哲学 | **zhéxué** | philosophy [5] |

zhēn
precious thing, treasure

Rad: 王   Str: 9

珍惜	**zhēnxī**	treasure, value, cherish [5]
珍贵	**zhēnguì**	valuable, precious [6]
珍稀	**zhēnxī**	rare, precious [6]
珍珠	**zhēnzhū**	pearl, genuine pearl [6]

zhěn
examine or treat medically

Rad: 讠   Str: 7

| 急诊 | **jízhěn** | emergency (e.g. hospital unit) [5] |
| 诊断 | **zhěnduàn** | diagnose, diagnosis [5] |

Additional words
诊所 **zhěnsuǒ** (clinic).

zhèn
disposition of troops, wave, burst, spell, measure word (for short periods of time)

Rad: 阝　Str: 6

阵	**zhèn**	short period of time, measure word (for events or state of a short duration) [5]
阵地	**zhèndì**	battlefront, front, ground, position [6]
阵容	**zhènróng**	line-up (of sports team etc.), troop arrangement [6]

Additional words
矩阵 **jǔzhèn** (matrix);
一阵风 **yí zhèn fēng** (a short period of time).

zhèn
rouse

Rad: 扌　Str: 10

振动	**zhèndòng**	to vibrate, vibration [5]
振奋	**zhènfèn**	to raise one's spirits, hearten [6]
振兴	**zhènxīng**	vitalise, develop, promote [6]

zhèn
shake, shock

Rad: 雨　Str: 15

地震	**dìzhèn**	earthquake [5]
震撼	**zhènhàn**	convulse, shock (wave) [6]
震惊	**zhènjīng**	astound [6]

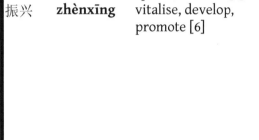

zhēng
attack, levy (troops or taxes), journey, trip, expedition

Rad: 彳　Str: 8

特征	**tèzhēng**	distinctive sign, characteristic, feature, trait [5]
象征	**xiàngzhēng**	to symbolise, signify, symbol, token [5]
征求	**zhēngqiú**	to ask for, seek, solicit [5]
征服	**zhēngfú**	to conquer, subjugate, subdue [6]
征收	**zhēngshōu**	to levy (a fine), to impose (a tariff) [6]

Additional words
长征 **cháng zhēng** (The Long March).

zhēng
to open (eye)

Rad: 目   Str: 11

| 睁 | **zhēng** | open (the eyes) [5] |

zhèng
politics, political,
government

Rad: 攵   Str: 9

政府	**zhèngfǔ**	government [5]
政治	**zhèngzhì**	politics, political [5]
财政	**cáizhèng**	government finance, public economy [6]
行政	**xíngzhèng**	administration, administrative [6]
政策	**zhèngcè**	policy [6]
政权	**zhèngquán**	political power, regime [6]

Additional words
专政 **zhuānzhèng** (dictatorship).

zhèng
struggle, to earn, to
make (money)

zhēng
struggle

Rad: 扌   Str: 9

| 挣 | **zhèng** | struggle to get free, try to break loose, earn, make [5] |
| 挣扎 | **zhēngzhá** | struggle, battle, flounder [6] |

zhī
weave

Rad: 纟   Str: 8

组织	**zǔzhī**	to organise, organisation [5]
编织	**biānzhī**	knit, weave [6]
纺织	**fǎngzhī**	spinning and weaving, textile [6]

zhí

execute (a plan), grasp

Rad: 扌   Str: 6

执照	**zhízhào**	licence, permit [5]
固执	**gùzhi**	stubborn [6]
执行	**zhíxíng**	to implement, carry out, execute, run [6]
执着	**zhízhe**	attached to, stubborn [6]

zhì

to rule, govern, manage, control, harness (a river), heal, cure, treatment, punish

Rad: 氵   Str: 8

政治	**zhèngzhì**	politics, political [5]
治疗	**zhìliáo**	to treat, to cure, medical treatment, cure [5]
防治	**fángzhì**	prevent and treat (diseases) [6]
统治	**tǒngzhì**	to rule, dominate [6]
治安	**zhì'ān**	law and order, public security [6]
治理	**zhìlǐ**	to govern, administer, manage, control [6]

zhì

to work out, system, control, dominate, manufacture

Rad: 刂   Str: 8

复制	**fùzhì**	to duplicate, make a copy of, reproduce, clone [5]
控制	**kòngzhì**	to control, dominate, command [5]
限制	**xiànzhì**	to confine, restrict, limit, restriction [5]
制定	**zhìdìng**	to establish, lay down, stipulate [5]
制度	**zhìdù**	system (e.g. political, administrative etc.), institution [5]
制造	**zhìzào**	to manufacture, to make [5]
制作	**zhìzuò**	produce, make, build, construct [5]
抵制	**dǐzhì**	to resist, to boycott, to refuse (to cooperate), resistance, refusal [6]
遏制	**èzhì**	to restrain, hold back [6]
节制	**jiézhì**	temperance, moderation [6]
克制	**kèzhì**	restraint, self-control [6]
牵制	**qiānzhì**	to control, to curb, to restrict, to pin down (enemy troops) [6]
强制	**qiángzhì**	to enforce, enforcement, forcibly, compulsory [6]
压制	**yāzhì**	to suppress, to inhibit, to stifle [6]
制裁	**zhìcái**	to punish, punishment, sanctions (incl. economic) [6]
制服	**zhìfú**	to subdue, to check, to bring under control, uniform (army, party, school etc.) [6]
制约	**zhìyuē**	restrict [6]
制止	**zhìzhǐ**	to prevent, stop, curb, restrain, check, deter [6]

致 zhì
to send, to devote, to deliver, to cause, to convey, fine and close

Rad: 至   Str: 10

导致	**dǎozhì**	to lead to, bring about, result in, cause [5]
一致	**yízhì**	unanimous, consistent, identical (views or opinions) [5]
别致	**biézhì**	unusual, unique [6]
大致	**dàzhì**	general, rough, overall [6]
精致	**jīngzhì**	fine, exquisite, delicate, refined [6]
细致	**xìzhì**	attentive to detail, rich in detail [6]
兴致勃勃	**xìngzhìbóbó**	in high spirits [6]
以致	**yǐzhì**	so that, as a result, consequently [6]
致辞	**zhìcí**	oration, to address (an audience) [6]
致力	**zhìlì**	devote one's efforts to, dedication [6]
致使	**zhìshǐ**	to cause, to result in [6]

Additional words
雅致 **yǎzhi** (elegant).

智 zhì
wisdom, knowledge

Rad: 日   Str: 12

智慧	**zhìhuì**	wisdom, knowledge, intelligence, intelligent [5]
机智	**jīzhì**	tactful, resourceful [6]
理智	**lǐzhì**	intellect, reason [6]
明智	**míngzhì**	sensible, reasonable [6]
智力	**zhìlì**	intellect, intelligence [6]
智能	**zhìnéng**	intelligent, able, smart (phone, system, bomb etc.) [6]
智商	**zhìshāng**	IQ [6]

秩 zhì
order, orderliness

Rad: 禾   Str: 10

| 秩序 | **zhìxù** | order, orderly state [5] |

置 **zhì**
to install, to place, to put

Rad: 罒   Str: 13

位置	**wèizhì**	place, position, seat [5]
安置	**ānzhì**	to find a place for, help settle down, put, arrange for [6]
布置	**bùzhì**	to fix up, arrange, decorate [6]
处置	**chǔzhì**	to handle, to take care of, to punish [6]
设置	**shèzhì**	to set up, to install [6]

 骤 **zhòu**
sudden, suddenly

Rad: 马   Str: 17

| 步骤 | **bùzhòu** | step, move, measure, procedure [5] |

 猪 **zhū**
pig

Rad: 犭   Str: 11

| 猪 | **zhū** | pig, hog, swine [5] |

Additional words
猪年 **zhūnián** (the year of the pig (the 12th year)).

 竹 **zhú**
bamboo

Rad: 竹   Str: 6

| 竹子 | **zhúzi** | bamboo [5] |
| 烟花爆竹 | **yānhuābàozhú** | fireworks and crackers [6] |

Additional words
爆竹 **bàozhú** (firecracker).

zhú

to pursue, to chase,
individually, one by one

Rad: 辶   Str: 10

逐步	**zhúbù**	step by step, gradually [5]
逐渐	**zhújiàn**	gradually, by degrees [5]
驱逐	**qūzhú**	drive out, banish [6]
逐年	**zhúnián**	year after year, with each passing year, over the years [6]

zhǔ

to cook, to boil

Rad: 灬   Str: 12

| 煮 | **zhǔ** | cook, boil [5] |

zhù

build

Rad: 竹   Str: 12

| 建筑 | **jiànzhù** | to build, construct, architecture, building [5] |

Additional words
建筑学 **jiànzhùxué** (architecture).

zhuā

to grab, to catch, to
arrest, to snatch

Rad: 扌   Str: 7

| 抓 | **zhuā** | seize, grab, catch, scratch, stress [5] |
| 抓紧 | **zhuājǐn** | firmly grasp, pay close attention to [5] |

zhuāng
adornment, adorn, costume, dress, clothing

Rad: 衣   Str: 12

安装	**ānzhuāng**	install, erect, fix, mount, installation [5]
服装	**fúzhuāng**	dress, clothing, costume, clothes [5]
假装	**jiǎzhuāng**	to pretend, feign [5]
装	**zhuāng**	to act, pretend, load, assemble, fit [5]
装饰	**zhuāngshì**	decorate, adorn, ornament, accessory [5]
装修	**zhuāngxiū**	fix, install [5]
包装	**bāozhuāng**	pack, package [6]
武装	**wǔzhuāng**	weaponry, arm forces, arm, equip [6]
装备	**zhuāngbèi**	equipment, to equip, to outfit [6]
装卸	**zhuāngxiè**	to load and unload [6]

zhuàng
accusation, suit, state, condition, strong, great

Rad: 犬   Str: 7

形状	**xíngzhuàng**	shape, figure, form [5]
状况	**zhuàngkuàng**	state of affairs, condition [5]
状态	**zhuàngtài**	state, condition [5]
现状	**xiànzhuàng**	status quo [6]
症状	**zhèngzhuàng**	symptom [6]

zhuàng
to hit, to strike, to meet by accident, to run into, to bump against, to bump into

Rad: 扌   Str: 15

| 撞 | **zhuàng** | collide, bump against, run into [5] |

zhuī
pursue (a problem), to chase

Rad: 辶   Str: 9

追	**zhuī**	run after, pursue, trace, go after [5]
追求	**zhuīqiú**	to pursue, seek, woo, run after (a woman) [5]
追悼	**zhuīdào**	mourning, memorial service [6]
追究	**zhuījiū**	to investigate, find out [6]

zī
consult

Rad: 口   Str: 9

咨询   **zīxún**   refer, consult [5]

姿

zī
beauty, disposition, looks, appearance

Rad: 女   Str: 9

姿势   **zīshì**   posture, gesture, pose, carriage [5]
姿态   **zītài**   carriage, bearing, attitude, gesture [6]

zǐ
purple

Rad: 糸   Str: 12

紫   **zǐ**   purple [5]

综

zōng
to sum up

Rad: 纟   Str: 11

综合   **zōnghé**   to synthesise, integrate [5]

zǔ

to hinder, to block, to obstruct

Rad: 阝　Str: 7

阻止	**zǔzhǐ**	to prevent, block, stop [5]
阻碍	**zǔ'ài**	impede, hinder, block, obstacle, hindrance [6]
阻拦	**zǔlán**	to stop, obstruct [6]
阻挠	**zǔnáo**	obstruct, stand in the way [6]

zǔ

to form, compose, make up, group, to organize

Rad: 纟　Str: 8

组	**zǔ**	to form, to organise, group, team [5]
组成	**zǔchéng**	form, compose, constitute, make [5]
组合	**zǔhé**	to assemble [5]
组织	**zǔzhī**	to organise, organisation [5]

zuì

intoxicated

Rad: 酉　Str: 15

醉	**zuì**	become drunk, be tipsy [5]
麻醉	**mázuì**	anaesthetise [6]
陶醉	**táozuì**	intoxicate, intoxication [6]

遵

zūn

to observe, to obey, to follow

Rad: 辶　Str: 15

| 遵守 | **zūnshǒu** | to comply with, abide by, respect (an agreement) [5] |
| 遵循 | **zūnxún** | follow, keep to [6] |

CODE for additional learning resources
Hsk5dD8q

Appendix 1: Additional Level 5 Words

This book includes all characters which are new in level 5. However, there are some level 4 wordswhich use characters from levels 1 to 4, and are not in the pages above. They are listed below (**551 in total**), together with the levels their characters occur.

Word	Pinyin	Meaning	Level(s)
爱护	àihù	to cherish, treasure, take good care of	1-3
爱惜	àixī	to cherish, treasure, use sparingly	1-4
爱心	àixīn	compassion	1-3
办理	bànlǐ	to handle, conduct, deal with	3-3
保持	bǎochí	to keep, maintain, preserve	4-4
保存	bǎocún	to conserve, to preserve, to keep, to save (a file etc. in a computer)	4-4
保留	bǎoliú	to reserve, hold back, reservations	4-3
保险	bǎoxiǎn	insurance, to insure, safe, secure, be sure	4-4
报到	bàodào	report for duty, check in, register	2-2
报道	bàodào	report, cover, coverage, story	2-2
报告	bàogào	to make known, report, speech, lecture	2-2
报社	bàoshè	newspaper office	2-4
被子	bèizi	quilt	3-1
本科	běnkē	undergraduate (course)	1-4
本质	běnzhì	essence, nature	1-4
比例	bǐlì	proportion	2-4
必然	bìrán	inevitable, certain	3-2
必要	bìyào	necessary, essential, indispensable	3-2
毕竟	bìjìng	after all, when all is said and done, in the end	4-4
便	biàn	ordinary, plain, convenient, handy, easy, so, thus, to relieve oneself, to urinate, to defecate, then, in that case, even if, soon afterwards	2
标点	biāodiǎn	punctuation, a punctuation mark, to punctuate	4-1
标志	biāozhì	indicate, mark, sign, symbol	4-4
表面	biǎomiàn	surface, outside, face, appearance	2-1
表明	biǎomíng	to make clear, to make known, to state clearly, to indicate, known	2-1
表情	biǎoqíng	expression (facial)	2-2
表现	biǎoxiàn	show off, express, display	2-1
播放	bōfàng	to broadcast, to transmit	4-3
博物馆	bówùguǎn	museum	4-3-2
不安	bù'ān	uneasy, disturbed	1-3

不得了	bùdéliǎo	extremely, exceedingly, disastrous	1-2-1
不断	búduàn	unceasing, continuous	1-4
不见得	bújiàndé	not necessarily, not likely	1-1-2
不耐烦	búnàifán	impatient, impatience	1-4-4
不然	bùrán	otherwise	1-2
不如	bùrú	not as good as, better to	1-3
不要紧	búyàojǐn	doesn't matter	1-2-4
不足	bùzú	not enough, insufficient, inadequate	1-2
部门	bùmén	department, branch, section, division	4-2
参考	cānkǎo	refer to, consult	3-2
参与	cānyù	to participate (in sth)	3-4
差距	chājù	disparity, distance	3-4
常识	chángshí	common sense, general knowledge	2-1
超级	chāojí	transcending, high grade, super-, ultra-	3-3
成分	chéngfèn	ingredient	3-1
成果	chéngguǒ	gain, achievement, positive result	3-1
成就	chéngjiù	achievement, success	3-2
成人	chéngrén	adult	3-1
成熟	chéngshú	mature, ripe	3-4
成语	chéngyǔ	idiom, proverb, adage (Chinese set expression often made up of 4 characters or two couplets of 4 characters each, often alluding to a story or historical quotation)	3-1
成长	chéngzhǎng	to grow up	3-2
程度	chéngdù	degree, extent, level	4-4
程序	chéngxù	procedure, process, computer program	4-4
迟早	chízǎo	sooner or later	3-2
持续	chíxù	to continue, persist, last out	4-4
抽象	chōuxiàng	abstract	4-4
出口	chūkǒu	exit	1-3
出色	chūsè	excellent, outstanding	1-2
出示	chūshì	produce, production	1-4
除非	chúfēi	unless, barring, only if	3-2
处理	chǔlǐ	to handle, deal with	4-3
传播	chuánbō	to disseminate, to propagate, to spread	4-4
传染	chuánrǎn	to infect, be contagious	4-4
传说	chuánshuō	pass on (a story), people say, legend, folk tale	4-1
此外	cǐwài	besides, moreover	4-2

次要	cìyào	secondary, less important, subordinate, minor	2-2
从此	cóngcǐ	from now on	2-4
从而	cóng'ér	thus, thereby	2-3
从前	cóngqián	before, formerly, in the past	2-1
从事	cóngshì	to go for, engage in, undertake, deal with, handle, do	2-2
存在	cúnzài	exist, be	4-1
答应	dāying	to promise, to agree, to reply, to respond	3-3
打工	dǎgōng	to work (do manual labour for a living)	1-1
打交道	dǎjiāodao	come into contact with, have dealings with	1-4-2
打听	dǎting	to ask about, inquire about	1-1
大方	dàfang	of good taste, generous, natural and poised	1-3
大象	dàxiàng	elephant	1-4
担任	dānrèn	assume the office of, hold the post of	3-4
单调	dāndiào	monotonous, dull	3-3
单位	dānwèi	unit (of measure), work unit (one's workplace)	3-3
单元	dānyuán	unit, entrance number, staircase (for residential buildings)	3-3
当地	dāngdì	local	3-3
当心	dāngxīn	to take care, look out	3-3
导演	dǎoyǎn	director, to direct (film etc.)	4-4
道理	dàolǐ	principle, truth, reason, argument	2-3
的确	díquè	indeed, really	1-4
登记	dēngjì	to register, check in	4-3
等于	děngyú	equal to, equivalent, amount to	2-3
地道	dìdao	genuine, real, authentic, pure, up to standard	3-2
地理	dìlǐ	geography, the natural and social features of a place	3-3
地区	dìqū	area, region, district	3-4
地位	dìwèi	position, status	3-3
点心	diǎnxin	light refreshments, pastry, dim sum (in Cantonese cooking), dessert	1-3
电台	diàntái	transceiver, broadcasting station	1-4
动画片	dònghuàpiàn	cartoon, animated film	2-3-3
度过	dùguò	spend, pass	4-2
断	duàn	to break, snap, cut off, sever, judge (usu negative)	4
对比	duìbǐ	compare, contrast, comparison	1-2
对方	duìfāng	other person involved, receiving party	1-3
对手	duìshǒu	rival, adversary, opponent	1-2
对象	duìxiàng	object, target, boyfriend or girlfriend	1-4

朵	duǒ	measure word (for flowers, clouds)	3
耳环	ěrhuán	earring	3-3
发表	fābiǎo	publish, issue	3-2
发明	fāmíng	invent, invention	3-1
发票	fāpiào	invoice, receipt	3-2
发言	fāyán	speak, make a speech	3-4
法院	fǎyuàn	court (of law)	3-1
翻	fān	to turn over, flip over, capsize, translate	4
反而	fǎn'ér	on the contrary, instead	4-3
反复	fǎnfù	repeatedly, again and again	4-3
反应	fǎnyìng	react, respond, reaction, response	4-3
反正	fǎnzhèng	anyway, in any case	4-2
方	fāng	side, square, direction, party (to a contract, dispute etc.), measure word (for square things)	3
方案	fāng'àn	scheme, plan, program	3-4
方式	fāngshì	way, fashion, pattern	3-4
非	fēi	not, non-, un-, insist on, simply must	2
分别	fēnbié	to separate, distinguish, respectively	1-2
分手	fēnshǒu	to break up, separate	1-2
风格	fēnggé	style	3-4
风景	fēngjǐng	scenery, landscape	3-4
风险	fēngxiǎn	risk, venture	3-4
否定	fǒudìng	to negate, deny	4-3
否认	fǒurèn	to deny	4-1
改进	gǎijìn	to improve, make better, improvement	4-2
改正	gǎizhèng	correct, amend	4-2
赶紧	gǎnjǐn	hurriedly, on the double, lose no time	4-4
赶快	gǎnkuài	at once, quickly	4-2
感激	gǎnjī	to express thanks, grateful, moved to gratitude	3-4
感受	gǎnshòu	be affected by, taste, feel, experience, feeling	3-4
感想	gǎnxiǎng	impressions, reflections	3-1
干活儿	gànhuór	to work, manual labour	3-4-1
钢铁	gāngtiě	steel	4-3
高级	gāojí	higher-grade, high-quality, advanced, high-ranking	1-3
告别	gàobié	leave, part from, say goodbye to	2-2
格外	géwài	especially, particularly, all the more	4-2
个别	gèbié	respective, respectively, individual	1-2

个人	gèrén	individual, personal, oneself	1-1
个性	gèxìng	personality, individuality, character	1-4
各自	gèzì	each, respective	4-3
根	gēn	root, foot, base, origin, measure word (for long slender objects, e.g. cigarettes, guitar strings)	3
根本	gēnběn	root, essence, basic, fundamental	3-1
工程师	gōngchéngshī	engineer	1-4-1
工具	gōngjù	tool	1-4
工人	gōngrén	worker, workman	1-1
工业	gōngyè	industry	1-3
公开	gōngkāi	in public, overt, open, make public	2-1
公平	gōngpíng	fair, impartial	2-3
公元	gōngyuán	the Christian era, AD	2-3
公主	gōngzhǔ	princess	2-3
功能	gōngnéng	function, functionality, feature	4-1
鼓舞	gǔwǔ	heartening (news), boost (morale)	4-2
挂号	guàhào	to register (a letter, hospital appointment etc.)	4-1
怪不得	guàibude	no wonder, so that's why, put no blame on	3-1-2
观察	guānchá	to observe, to watch, to survey, to examine, observation, view, perspective	4-4
观点	guāndiǎn	viewpoint, standpoint	4-1
管子	guǎnzi	tube, pipe, drinking straw	4-1
光明	guāngmíng	light, bright	4-1
光盘	guāngpán	CD	4-3
广场	guǎngchǎng	public square, plaza	4-2
广大	guǎngdà	extensive, vast, wide	4-1
规律	guīlǜ	law, regular pattern, rule (e.g. of science)	4-4
规则	guīzé	rule, law, regulation, regular, orderly	4-4
果然	guǒrán	as expected, really, sure enough	1-2
果实	guǒshí	fruit, gains	1-3
过分	guòfèn	excessive, undue, extravagant	2-1
过期	guòqī	outdated, beyond sell-by date	2-1
海关	hǎiguān	customs	4-1
海鲜	hǎixiān	seafood	4-3
行动	xíngdòng	to move, act, action	3-2
行人	xíngrén	pedestrian	3-1
行为	xíngwéi	act, action, behaviour, conduct	3-2
行业	hángyè	trade, business, industry	3-3

好客	hàokè	hospitable	1-1
好奇	hàoqí	curious, inquisitive	1-3
合法	héfǎ	legal, lawful, legitimate, rightful	4-3
合理	hélǐ	reasonable, rational	4-3
合同	hétong	contract (in business, work etc.)	4-1
合影	héyǐng	group photo	4-1
合作	hézuò	to cooperate, collaborate, work together, cooperation	4-1
何必	hébì	why is it necessary to, there is no need to	4-3
何况	hékuàng	let alone (used in rhetorical questions)	4-4
和平	hépíng	peace	1-3
后果	hòuguǒ	consequence, aftermath	1-1
呼吸	hūxī	to breathe	4-4
花生	huāshēng	peanut	3-1
划	huá	to row, delimit, transfer, assign, differentiate, mark off, draw (a line), delete, stroke of a Chinese character	4
化学	huàxué	chemistry	3-1
话题	huàtí	subject (of a talk or conversation), topic	1-2
黄金	huángjīn	gold	3-4
会计	kuàijì	accountant, accountancy	1-4
婚礼	hūnlǐ	wedding ceremony	3-3
或许	huòxǔ	perhaps, maybe	3-4
基本	jīběn	basic, fundamental, on the whole	4-1
及格	jígé	to pass a test or exam	4-4
极其	jíqí	most, extremely, exceedingly	3-3
急忙	jímáng	hastily	3-2
计算	jìsuàn	to count, to calculate, to compute	4-3
记忆	jìyì	remember, memory	3-4
纪律	jìlǜ	rule, discipline	4-4
家务	jiāwù	housework	1-2
假如	jiǎrú	if, supposing, in case, in the event that	3-3
价值	jiàzhí	worth, value	4-4
坚决	jiānjué	firm, resolute, determined	4-3
简历	jiǎnlì	CV, resume	3-3
简直	jiǎnzhí	simply, utterly, totally, at all, virtually	3-3
健身	jiànshēn	body-building	3-2
键盘	jiànpán	keyboard (piano or typewriter)	4-3
讲究	jiǎngjiu	be particular about, exquisite, tasteful, elegant	3-4

讲座	jiǎngzuò	course of lectures	3-4
交换	jiāohuàn	to exchange, to swap	4-3
交际	jiāojì	communication, social intercourse	4-4
交往	jiāowǎng	association, contact, to affiliate with	4-2
角度	jiǎodù	angle, perspective, point of view	3-4
角色	juésè	role, part (in a play etc), character (in a novel etc)	3-2
教材	jiàocái	teaching materials	2-4
教练	jiàoliàn	coach, instructor, drill master	2-3
接近	jiējìn	be close to, near	3-2
节省	jiéshěng	economise, save	3-4
结合	jiéhé	to combine, unite, integrate, link	3-4
结论	jiélùn	conclusion, verdict	3-4
结实	jiēshi	solid, sturdy	3-3
借口	jièkǒu	to use as an excuse, on the pretext	3-3
紧急	jǐnjí	urgent, pressing	4-3
尽快	jǐnkuài	as soon as possible	4-2
尽力	jìnlì	try one's best, do all one can	4-3
尽量	jǐnliàng	as much as possible, to the greatest extent	4-4
进步	jìnbù	advance, progress, improve, progressive	2-2
进口	jìnkǒu	to import, imported	2-3
经典	jīngdiǎn	classics, scriptures	2-3
经商	jīngshāng	be in business, trade	2-1
精力	jīnglì	energy, vigour	4-3
酒吧	jiǔbā	bar, pub	3-2
居然	jūrán	unexpectedly, to one's surprise, go so far as to	3-2
具备	jùbèi	to possess, have, be provided with	4-2
具体	jùtǐ	concrete, specific, particular	4-2
据说	jùshuō	it is said that, reportedly	3-1
决赛	juésài	final (of a competition)	3-3
决心	juéxīn	be determined, determination	3-3
绝对	juéduì	absolute	4-1
卡车	kǎchē	lorry, truck	3-1
开发	kāifā	to exploit (a resource), open up (for development), to develop	1-3
开放	kāifàng	to lift (a ban or restriction), to open to the outside world (politics), to open for public use	1-3
开水	kāishuǐ	boiled water, boiling water	1-1
看不起	kànbuqǐ	look down on, despise	1-1-1

看望	kànwàng	to call on, visit, see	1-2
可见	kějiàn	it is thus obvious that, we can see that, it shows that	2-1
可怕	kěpà	fearful, terrible, frightful, horrible	2-3
克	kè	gram, to subdue, to restrain	4
克服	kèfú	to overcome (hardships etc), to conquer, to put up with, to endure	4-1
刻苦	kèkǔ	assiduous, hardworking	3-4
客观	kèguān	objectivity, objective	1-4
课程	kèchéng	course, class	2-4
空间	kōngjiān	space	3-2
口味	kǒuwèi	flavour, a person's tastes or preferences (in food)	3-4
老百姓	lǎobǎixìng	ordinary people, the man in the street	1-2-2
老板	lǎobǎn	boss	1-3
老实	lǎoshi	frank, honest	1-3
乐观	lèguān	optimistic, hopeful	2-4
了不起	liǎobuqǐ	great, extraordinary	1-1-1
离婚	líhūn	to divorce, be divorced	2-3
理论	lǐlùn	theory	3-4
理由	lǐyóu	reason, grounds, justification	3-4
力量	lìliàng	power, force	3-4
利息	lìxī	accrual, interest (on a loan)	4-2
利用	lìyòng	use, utilise, exploit, make use of	4-3
连忙	liánmáng	promptly, at once	4-2
连续	liánxù	continually, in succession	4-4
联合	liánhé	to combine, to join, unite, alliance	4-4
亮	liàng	bright, shiny, light, to show, shine	1
列车	lièchē	train	4-1
零件	língjiàn	part, component	2-2
流传	liúchuán	to spread, circulate, hand down, pass down	4-4
论文	lùnwén	treatise, paper, thesis	4-3
落后	luòhòu	backward, fall behind	4-1
满足	mǎnzú	satisfied, contented	3-2
毛病	máobìng	fault, defect, shortcoming	4-2
冒险	màoxiǎn	take a risk	3-4
美术	měishù	fine arts, art	4-4
梦想	mèngxiǎng	to dream of, hope vainly, wishful thinking	4-1
密切	mìqiè	intimate, close, carefully, be close	4-4

面对	miànduì	face, confront, meet	1-1
面积	miànjī	area	1-4
名牌	míngpái	famous brand	1-4
名片	míngpiàn	business card	1-3
明确	míngquè	to clarify, clear-cut	1-4
明星	míngxīng	star, celebrity	1-1
命运	mìngyùn	fate, destiny	4-2
目标	mùbiāo	target, goal, objective	3-4
目前	mùqián	current time, at present	3-1
哪怕	nǎpà	even if	1-3
难怪	nánguài	it's no wonder that, it's not surprising that	3-3
难免	nánmiǎn	hard to avoid	3-4
脑袋	nǎodai	head, brains, mental ability	1-4
内部	nèibù	internal, inside	4-4
内科	nèikē	internal medicine (hospital dept using drugs vs. surgery)	4-4
能干	nénggàn	able, capable, competent	1-3
年纪	niánjì	age	1-4
牛仔裤	niúzǎikù	jeans	2-4-3
女士	nǚshì	lady, madam	1-4
偶然	ǒurán	accidental, fortuitous, unexpected	4-2
批	pī	to ascertain, to act on, to criticise, to pass on, measure word (for batches, lots, military flights)	4
批准	pīzhǔn	to ratify, approve	4-2
片	piàn	thin piece, flake, slice, measure word (for slices, tablets, tract of land, area of water, CDs, movies, DVDs, scenario, scene, feeling, atmosphere, sound etc.)	3
片面	piànmiàn	unilateral, one-sided	3-1
平	píng	flat, level, equal, to tie (make the same score), to draw (score), calm, peaceful	3
平安	píng'ān	safe and sound	3-3
平常	píngcháng	generally, usually, ordinary, common	3-2
平等	píngděng	equal, equality	3-2
平方	píngfāng	square (foot, mile, root etc.)	3-3
平静	píngjìng	calm, quiet, tranquil	3-3
评价	píngjià	to evaluate, asses, evaluation	4-4
破坏	pòhuài	to ruin, destroy, destruction, damage	4-3
期间	qījiān	time, period	1-2

汽油	qìyóu	gasoline, petrol	2-4
签	qiān	sign one's name	4
切	qiē	to cut, to slice	4
亲爱	qīn'ài	dear, beloved (way of starting a letter)	4-1
亲切	qīnqiè	cordial, kind	4-4
亲自	qīnzì	personally	4-3
轻视	qīngshì	look down upon, despise, belittle, underestimate	3-1
轻易	qīngyì	lightly and easily, lightly, easily	3-3
情景	qíngjǐng	scene, sight	2-4
请求	qǐngqiú	request, ask for sth	1-3
球迷	qiúmí	football fan, crazy about sports	2-4
取消	qǔxiāo	to cancel, call off	4-4
去世	qùshì	to pass away, die	1-3
全面	quánmiàn	overall, all-round, comprehensive	4-1
确定	quèdìng	to make certain, make sure, definite, certain, fixed, to determine, OK (on computer pop-up)	4-3
确认	quèrèn	to confirm	4-1
热爱	rè'ài	to love ardently, adore	1-1
热心	rèxīn	enthusiastic, ardent	1-3
人才	réncái	talented person	1-3
人口	rénkǒu	population	1-3
人生	rénshēng	human life	1-1
人事	rénshì	human affairs, ways of the world	1-2
人物	rénwù	figure, character (in a play, novel etc.)	1-3
人员	rényuán	personnel, staff	1-2
日常	rìcháng	daily, everyday	2-2
日程	rìchéng	schedule, itinerary	2-4
日历	rìlì	calendar	2-3
日期	rìqī	date	2-1
日子	rìzi	days, date, time, life, livelihood	2-1
如何	rúhé	how, what	3-4
如今	rújīn	nowadays, now	3-1
色彩	sècǎi	colour, hue, flavour, appeal	2-4
伤害	shānghài	hurt, harm, damage, injure, wound	4-3
商务	shāngwù	commerce, business	1-2
商业	shāngyè	commerce, trade, business	1-3
上当	shàngdàng	be fooled, be taken in	1-3

身材	shēncái	stature, build (height and weight), figure	2-4
身份	shēnfèn	identity, status	2-4
深刻	shēnkè	deep, profound	4-3
生动	shēngdòng	vivid, lively	1-2
生长	shēngzhǎng	to grow, grow up	1-2
声调	shēngdiào	tone, the tone of Chinese character	3-3
失去	shīqù	to lose	4-1
失业	shīyè	lose one's job, unemployment	4-3
时差	shíchā	time difference, jet lag	1-3
时刻	shíkè	moment	1-3
时期	shíqī	period (in time or history)	1-1
实话	shíhuà	truthful words, truth	3-1
实习	shíxí	practice, praxis, exercise and learn in the real world	3-1
实现	shíxiàn	realise, achieve, bring about	3-1
实验	shíyàn	experiment, test	3-4
实用	shíyòng	practical, pragmatic, applied (science)	3-3
始终	shǐzhōng	from beginning to end	2-3
市场	shìchǎng	market place, market	3-2
事实	shìshí	fact	2-3
事物	shìwù	thing, object	2-3
事先	shìxiān	in advance, beforehand	2-1
收获	shōuhuò	gain, harvest	4-4
收据	shōujù	receipt, voucher	4-3
手工	shǒugōng	handwork, manual	2-1
手术	shǒushù	operation, surgical operation	2-4
手续	shǒuxù	procedures	2-4
手指	shǒuzhǐ	finger	2-4
首	shǒu	head, first, leader, measure word (for songs)	4
受伤	shòushāng	to sustain injuries, wounded (in an accident etc), harmed	4-4
舒适	shūshì	comfortable, cosy, snug	3-4
输入	shūrù	to import, input	4-4
熟练	shúliàn	skilled, practiced, proficient	4-3
数	shǔ	number, figure, plan, to count, calculate, several, frequently, repeatedly	3
数据	shùjù	data	3-3
数码	shùmǎ	number, numeral	3-4
双方	shuāngfāng	both sides, the two parties	3-3

说不定	shuōbudìng	cannot say for sure, maybe, perhaps	1-1-3
说服	shuōfú	persuade, convince	1-1
思考	sīkǎo	to think over, ponder over, reflect upon, consider	2-2
思想	sīxiǎng	thought, thinking, idea, ideology	2-1
随身	suíshēn	to carry on one's person, to take with one	4-2
随时	suíshí	at any time, at all time	4-1
随手	suíshǒu	without extra trouble	4-2
所	suǒ	place, measure word (for houses, small buildings, institutions etc.)	2
太太	tàitai	wife, Mrs.	1-1
谈判	tánpàn	to negotiate	4-4
讨价还价	tǎojiàhuánjià	to haggle over price	4-4-2-4
特色	tèsè	characteristic, distinguishing feature or quality	3-2
疼爱	téngài	to love dearly	3-1
提问	tíwèn	to question, raise a question (in a class or meeting)	3-2
题目	tímù	title, subject	2-3
体会	tǐhuì	realise, know (through learning or experience)	2-1
体现	tǐxiàn	embody, incarnate	2-1
体验	tǐyàn	to experience for oneself	2-4
天空	tiānkōng	sky, heavens	1-3
天真	tiānzhēn	naïve, innocent	1-2
调皮	tiáopí	playful, naughty, mischievous, disobedient (e.g. child)	3-3
调整	tiáozhěng	to adjust, regulate, revise	3-4
通常	tōngcháng	usual, general, normal	4-2
突出	tūchū	outstanding, stand out	3-1
推广	tuīguǎng	popularise, spread	4-4
外公	wàigōng	maternal grandfather	2-2
外交	wàijiāo	diplomacy, foreign affairs	2-4
完美	wánměi	perfect	2-4
完整	wánzhěng	complete, intact	2-4
玩具	wánjù	toy	2-4
万一	wànyī	one in a thousand, eventuality, in case	3-1
危害	wēihài	endanger, jeopardise, harm	4-3
微笑	wēixiào	smile	4-2
围巾	wéijīn	scarf, muffler, shawl	4-4
位于	wèiyú	lie on, be located in, be situated in	3-3

温暖	wēnnuǎn	warm	4-4
文件	wénjiàn	document	3-2
文具	wénjù	stationery, item of stationery (pen, pencil, eraser, pencil sharpener etc.)	3-4
文明	wénmíng	civilisation, civilised	3-1
文学	wénxué	literature	3-1
文字	wénzì	character	3-1
闻	wén	to hear, smell, news	3
问候	wènhòu	to give one's respects, to send a greeting	2-1
无数	wúshù	innumerable, countless	4-3
物理	wùlǐ	physics	3-3
物质	wùzhì	matter, substance, material	3-4
吸取	xīqǔ	to absorb, to draw (a lesson, insight etc), to assimilate	4-4
吸收	xīshōu	to absorb, to assimilate, to ingest	4-4
戏剧	xìjù	drama, play, theatre	3-4
系	xì	department (in a university), to tie	1
细节	xìjié	detail, specific	4-3
现实	xiànshí	reality, actuality	1-3
现象	xiànxiàng	appearance, phenomenon	1-4
相处	xiāngchǔ	get along with each other	3-4
相当	xiāngdāng	equivalent to, appropriate, considerably, to a certain extent, fairly	3-3
相对	xiāngduì	face each other, be opposite, relative	3-1
相关	xiāngguān	correlate, correlation	3-1
想象	xiǎngxiàng	to imagine, to fancy	1-4
消费	xiāofèi	to consume, consumption, expense	4-4
消化	xiāohuà	digest, digestion	4-3
消极	xiāojí	negative, passive, inactive	4-3
消失	xiāoshī	to disappear, vanish	4-4
小气	xiǎoqi	mean, stingy, penny-pinching	1-1
写作	xiězuò	writing, written works	1-1
心理	xīnlǐ	psychology, mentality, thought, psychological	3-3
心脏	xīnzàng	heart	3-4
信号	xìnhào	signal	3-1
信任	xìnrèn	to trust, confide in, depend on, have faith in	3-4
幸运	xìngyùn	fortunate, lucky, fortune, luck	4-2
性质	xìngzhì	quality, nature, character	4-4
修改	xiūgǎi	to revise, modify, revision, modification	4-4

学历	xuélì	educational background	1-3
学术	xuéshù	systematic learning, science	1-4
学问	xuéwen	learning, knowledge, scholarship	1-2
演讲	yǎnjiǎng	give a lecture, make a speech	4-3
阳台	yángtái	balcony	3-4
样式	yàngshì	style, mode, manner	1-4
要不	yàobù	otherwise, or else, or	2-1
业务	yèwù	business, professional work	3-2
一律	yílǜ	without exception, same, uniformly	1-4
一再	yízài	repeatedly, again and again	1-1
疑问	yíwèn	doubt, query, question	4-2
以及	yǐjí	as well as, along with, and	2-4
以来	yǐlái	since (a previous event)	2-1
议论	yìlùn	to discuss, comment on	3-4
意外	yìwài	accidental, unexpected, accident	2-2
因而	yīn'ér	thus, as a result	2-3
银	yín	silver, silver-coloured, relating to money or currency	3
印刷	yìnshuā	print	4-3
迎接	yíngjiē	to welcome, greet, receive	3-3
影子	yǐngzi	shadow	1-1
应付	yìngfu	deal with, cope with, make do with	3-4
应用	yìngyòng	to use, apply, application, applicable	3-3
勇气	yǒngqì	courage	4-1
用功	yònggōng	hardworking, diligent	3-4
优美	yōuměi	fine, graceful	4-4
有利	yǒulì	advantageous, beneficial	1-4
与其	yǔqí	rather than, better than (usage: 与其... 不如... rather than..., better to...)	4-3
语气	yǔqì	tone, manner of speaking, mood	1-1
预报	yùbào	to predict, forecast, prediction	4-2
员工	yuángōng	employee, staff	2-1
原料	yuánliào	raw material	4-3
原则	yuánzé	principle, doctrine	4-4
愿望	yuànwàng	desire, wish, aspiration	3-2
运气	yùnqi	luck (good or bad)	2-1
运输	yùnshū	transport, haulage, transit	2-4
运用	yùnyòng	to utilise, apply	2-3

再三	zàisān	again and again, over and over again	1-1
在乎	zàihu	care about	1-3
在于	zàiyú	lie in, consist in, depend on, rest with	1-3
则	zé	then, in that case (conjunction used to express contrast with a previous clause), standard, norm	4
责备	zébèi	to blame, to criticize sb	4-2
展开	zhǎnkāi	to spread out, unfold, open up	4-1
占	zhàn	occupy, seize, take, constitute	4
照常	zhàocháng	as usual (business etc.)	3-2
着火	zhehuǒ	be on fire	2-2
着凉	zháoliáng	to catch a cold	2-4
针对	zhēnduì	be aimed at, be directed against	4-1
真实	zhēnshí	true, real, authentic	2-3
争论	zhēnglùn	to argue, debate, argument, contention	4-4
争取	zhēngqǔ	to fight for, to strive for, to win over	4-4
整个	zhěnggè	whole, entire	4-1
整体	zhěngtǐ	overall, whole, as a whole (situation, construction, team etc.), macrocosm	4-2
正	zhèng	upright, centrally located, exactly (of time or figure), correct	2
证件	zhèngjiàn	paperwork, credentials	4-2
证据	zhèngjù	evidence, proof, testimony	4-3
支	zhī	to support, sustain, erect, raise, branch, division, draw money, measure word (for rod-like things e.g. pens, pencils, guns, for army divisions, songs, power of light bulb)	4
支票	zhīpiào	cheque, check (bank)	4-2
直	zhí	straight, frank, straightforward, vertical, vertical downward stroke in Chinese characters	3
指导	zhǐdǎo	to guide, to give directions, to direct, to coach, guidance, tuition	4-4
至今	zhìjīn	up to now, to this day, so far	4-1
至于	zhìyú	as for, as to, to such an extent, to go so far as to	4-3
志愿者	zhìyuànzhě	volunteer, applicant	4-3-3
中介	zhōngjiè	agent, intermediary	1-2
中心	zhōngxīn	centre, heart	1-3
重大	zhòngdà	great, important, major, significant	3-1
重复	chóngfù	to repeat	3-3
重量	zhòngliàng	weight	3-4

周到	zhōudào	thoughtful, considerate	3-2
主持	zhǔchí	to take charge of, manage, direct, preside over, uphold, to stand for (e.g. justice), host (a TV or radio program etc.)	3-4
主动	zhǔdòng	to take the initiative, to do sth of one's own accord, active	3-2
主观	zhǔguān	subject, subjective thinking, subjective	3-4
主人	zhǔrén	master, host, owner	3-1
主任	zhǔrèn	director, head, chief	3-4
主题	zhǔtí	theme, subject, topic	3-2
主张	zhǔzhāng	to advocate, idea, view, proposition	3-3
祝福	zhùfú	bless, benediction	4-4
专家	zhuānjiā	expert, specialist	4-1
专心	zhuānxīn	be absorbed, attentive, concentrating	4-3
转变	zhuǎnbiàn	change, transform	4-3
转告	zhuǎngào	to pass on, to communicate, to transmit	4-2
资格	zīgé	qualifications	4-4
资金	zījīn	funds, money for business use, capital	4-4
资料	zīliào	material, resources, data, information	4-3
自从	zìcóng	since (a time), ever since	3-2
自动	zìdòng	automatic	3-2
自觉	zìjué	be aware of, conscious, conscientious	3-1
自由	zìyóu	freedom, liberty, free, unrestrained	3-4
自愿	zìyuàn	volunteer, be willing to	3-3
字母	zìmǔ	letter (of the alphabet)	1-4
总共	zǒnggòng	altogether, in all, in the aggregate, in total	3-2
总理	zǒnglǐ	premier, prime minister	3-3
总算	zǒngsuàn	at long last, finally, in the end, on the whole	3-3
总之	zǒngzhī	in short, in brief, in a nutshell, to sum up	3-4
作为	zuòwéi	regard as, take for, as	1-2
作文	zuòwén	write a composition, composition	1-3

Appendix 2: Measure Words

Measure words, also known as classifiers, are used with numerals or the words 这 **zhè** (this) and 那 **nà** (that) to qualify nouns. There are five types, as follows.

Type I. These are used with nouns, and are the most important type for Chinese learners. In general, these have no direct translation.

Type II. These are similar to Type I, but are used with verbs.

Type III. These describe containers of things, e.g. 杯 **bēi** (a cup).

Type IV. These are measure words with a general meaning. They are directly translatable. E.g. 点 **diǎn** (a little, a drop), 些 **xiē** (a number of, some).

Type V. These are used for units of measurement. Examples are 米 **mǐ** (metre), 天 **tiān** (day), and 岁 **suì** (years of age).

For more information on measure words, refer to Appendix 1 in *Chinese Characters for HSK: Level 1*.

The table below shows all the measure words which occur in Level 5, with their meaning, type and examples. There are a total of 13 measure words in HSK Level 5.

Char	Pinyin	Meaning	Type	Example
册	cè	for books	I	那册书 (volume (of a book))
顶	dǐng	for hats, headwear, veils	I	一顶帽子 (**màozi** hat)
顿	dùn	for meals, beatings, tellings off etc.	I	一顿吵架 (**chǎojià** argument)
幅	fú	for pictures, paintings, textile	I	一幅画 (**huà** painting)
股	gǔ	for electric current	I	一股泉水 (**quánshuǐ** (water) spring)
壶	hú	for bottle liquid	I	一壶水 (a pot of water)
架	jià	for planes, large vehicles, radios, etc.	I	一架飞机 (**fēijī** aeroplane)
届	jiè	for events, meetings, elections	I	这届政府 (**zhèngfǔ** government)
颗	kē	for small spheres, pearls, corn grains, teeth, hearts	I	一颗牙齿 (**yáchǐ** tooth)
匹	pǐ	for horses, mules, bolts of cloth	I	三匹马 (**mǎ** horses)
扇	shàn	for doors, windows, etc.	I	一扇门 (**mén** door)
套	tào	for sets, collections	I	一套水晶玻璃 (**shuǐjīng bōli** crystal wine glasses)
阵	zhèn	for short periods of time	I	一阵风 (**yí zhèn fēng** a short period of time)

English Index

Below is the index of characters according to their English meaning. To simplify the index, only the first part of the meaning of each character is used. If this is a verb, the base form (without 'to'), is used. Further, to avoid repetitions, only the first meaning is include for characters with more than one pronunciation.

boil	滚	gǔn	44	clip	夹	jiā	54
bone	骨	gǔ	42	clique	派	pài	86
book	册	cè	11	close	闭	bì	6
borrow	摘	zhāi	148	clown	丑	chǒu	19
brave	英	yīng	140	coal	煤	méi	78
break down	碎	suì	113	colored glaze	璃	lí	69
broad	泛	fàn	34	comb	梳	shū	109
build	筑	zhù	156	commerce	贸	mào	77
burn	燃	rán	97	compensate	偿	cháng	13
butterfly	蝶	dié	28	complicated	繁	fán	34
butterfly	蝴	hú	49	conceited	狂	kuáng	65
call	喊	hǎn	46	concentrated	浓	nóng	85
call together	召	zhào	150	conditions	势	shì	108
cannon	炮	pào	86	conduct	品	pǐn	90
carbon	炭	tàn	115	confine	圈	quān	96
carpenter's square	矩	jǔ	61	confused	晕	yūn	145
carry	载	zài	146	construct	构	gòu	41
carry on one's back	背	bèi	4	consult	咨	zī	158
cash	兑	duì	31	cook	煮	zhǔ	156
cause to be	令	lìng	73	copy	抄	chāo	14
cautious	谨	jǐn	60	court	庭	tíng	118
cautious	慎	shèn	105	cover	套	tào	117
cave	洞	dòng	29	cowries	贝	bèi	5
celebrate	庆	qìng	95	crafty	狡	jiǎo	58
chain	链	liàn	70	crisp	脆	cuì	23
chess	棋	qí	91	crooked	委	wěi	124
chest	胸	xiōng	133	cross-piece	档	dàng	27
China	华	huá	49	crouch	蹲	dūn	32
Chinese foot	尺	chǐ	17	crowd	群	qún	97
choose	挑	tiāo	118	crowded	挤	jǐ	53
chop	砍	kǎn	63	cultivate	培	péi	86
circle	圆	yuán	144	cupboard	柜	guì	44
clap	拍	pāi	85	curtain	帘	lián	70
cleanse	淘	táo	116	cut	裁	cái	9
clear	朗	lǎng	67	cut off	拦	lán	66
clear	浏	liú	73	damage	损	sǔn	113
clever	妙	miào	80	dark	暗	àn	2
cliff	厂	chǎng	14	dawn	旦	dàn	26

deal in	营	yíng	141
decay	腐	fǔ	38
declare	宣	xuān	134
deep fry	炸	zhá	148
deficiency	亏	kuī	65
deficient	欠	qiàn	93
delete	删	shān	101
demon	魅	mèi	78
depend upon	靠	kào	63
depict	描	miáo	80
descendant	昆	kūn	66
descendents	裔	yì	140
desert	漠	mò	81
detain in custody	押	yā	136
device	器	qì	92
devoid of content	虚	xū	133
difficult	艰	jiān	56
diffuse	布	bù	8
diligent	勤	qín	95
disaster	灾	zāi	146
disobey	违	wéi	123
disposition (troops)	阵	zhèn	151
dispute	辩	biàn	7
distribute	施	shī	106
district	县	xiàn	129
ditch	沟	gōu	41
do	搞	gǎo	39
do not	勿	wù	127
donate	捐	juān	62
double	兼	jiān	56
dragon	龙	lóng	74
drawer	屉	tì	117
dregs	糟	zāo	147
drive	驾	jià	55
drop	滴	dī	27
dry	燥	zào	147
dust	尘	chén	16
earnest	恳	kěn	64

earth	土	tǔ	120
elder brother	兄	xiōng	133
enclose	括	kuò	66
encroach	凌	líng	72
enemy	敌	dí	28
enjoy	享	xiǎng	130
enjoy beauty of	赏	shǎng	102
enlarge	扩	kuò	66
entirely	俱	jù	61
equal	均	jūn	62
escape	逃	táo	116
Europe	欧	ōu	85
even	齐	qí	91
even	匀	yún	145
evening	夕	xī	127
examine medically	诊	zhěn	150
excellent	嘉	jiā	54
execute	执	zhí	153
extra	余	yú	143
eyebrow	眉	méi	77
face	朝	cháo	14
face	临	lín	72
fan	扇	shàn	101
fantasy	幻	huàn	50
fashionable	髦	máo	77
favor	惠	huì	52
feast	宴	yàn	136
feel attached to	恋	liàn	70
feel with the hand	摸	mō	80
field	域	yù	144
fight	斗	dǒu	30
fight	战	zhàn	149
fight over	抢	qiǎng	94
filial	孝	xiào	131
fill	充	chōng	18
firewood	柴	chái	12
first in order	甲	jiǎ	54
first place	冠	guàn	43

fish (v)	钓	diào	28
fist	拳	quán	97
flash	闪	shǎn	101
flat	坦	tǎn	115
fling	甩	shuǎi	110
float	飘	piāo	89
fog	雾	wù	127
foolish	呆	dāi	24
foolish	傻	shǎ	100
footprint	迹	jì	54
force	迫	pò	91
fork	叉	chā	12
form	组	zǔ	159
freeze	冻	dòng	29
frequency	频	pín	89
frighten	吓	xià	128
fulfill	践	jiàn	57
funnel	漏	lòu	74
gall	胆	dǎn	26
gather	集	jí	53
gather	统	tǒng	118
gather round	拥	yōng	141
gather up	辑	jí	53
ghost	鬼	guǐ	44
give birth to	产	chǎn	13
glamorous	艳	yàn	137
glass	玻	bō	7
glory	荣	róng	98
glue	胶	jiāo	58
go around	绕	rào	98
go back	归	guī	44
good	良	liáng	70
good	善	shàn	102
grab	抓	zhuā	156
gradual	渐	jiàn	57
grain	颗	kē	63
grand	豪	háo	46
grandma	姥	lǎo	68

grandmother	婆	pó	90
gray	灰	huī	51
guard	守	shǒu	108
guiding principle	纲	gāng	39
gun	枪	qiāng	93
hair	毫	háo	46
hand over	递	dì	28
happy	欣	xīn	132
hard	固	gù	42
hard	硬	yìng	141
hasten	趋	qū	95
hasten	驶	shǐ	107
hate	恨	hèn	47
heroic	雄	xióng	133
hey	哎	āi	1
hide away	藏	cáng	10
hinder	碍	ài	1
hinder	挡	dǎng	26
hinder	妨	fáng	35
hinder	阻	zǔ	159
hit	击	jī	52
hit	撞	zhuàng	157
hold	操	cāo	10
hold in one's hand	托	tuō	121
honey	蜜	mì	79
hope for	盼	pàn	86
how can one help	奈	nài	83
huh	嗯	ńg	83
hundred million	亿	yì	139
hurried	匆	cōng	22
hurry	促	cù	22
imitate	仿	fǎng	35
imitate	模	mó	81
in charge of	掌	zhǎng	149
indulge	耽	dān	25
inferior	劣	liè	71
initiate	倡	chàng	14
inquire	访	fǎng	35

inquire	询	xún	135
insane	疯	fēng	36
insect	虫	chóng	18
insert	插	chā	12
insipid	淡	dàn	26
install	置	zhì	155
intelligent	慧	huì	52
intestines	肠	cháng	13
intoxicated	醉	zuì	159
island	岛	dǎo	27
islet	屿	yǔ	143
itch	痒	yǎng	137
jade	玉	yù	143
jewel	宝	bǎo	4
join	配	pèi	87
jump	跃	yuè	145
justice	义	yì	139
keen	敏	mǐn	80
keep	含	hán	45
kidnap	拐	guǎi	43
kill	杀	shā	100
kind	类	lèi	68
king	王	wáng	122
kiss	吻	wěn	125
knock against	触	chù	20
laughter	哈	hā	45
lean against	凭	píng	90
leather	革	gé	40
lend on interest	贷	dài	25
lenient	宽	kuān	65
lid	盖	gài	39
lie	卧	wò	126
lifetime	辈	bèi	5
limit	限	xiàn	129
linger	逗	dòu	30
lion	狮	shī	106
lock	锁	suǒ	114
lodge for the night	宿	sù	112

logic	逻	luó	75
lonesome	寂	jì	53
lonesome	寞	mò	82
long life	寿	shòu	108
look at	瞧	qiáo	94
look over	览	lǎn	67
lose	遗	yí	138
lose in trade	赔	péi	87
love	宠	chǒng	19
make	造	zào	147
marriage	姻	yīn	140
marry	嫁	jià	55
martial	武	wǔ	126
mate	匹	pǐ	89
maternal uncle	舅	jiù	61
mean	薄	báo	4
medium	媒	méi	78
melt	销	xiāo	131
miasma	氛	fēn	36
model	型	xíng	132
modest	谦	qiān	92
moist	湿	shī	106
money	币	bì	6
money	财	cái	9
monkey	猴	hóu	48
mother	娘	niáng	84
move	移	yí	139
muddled	糊	hú	49
muscle	肌	jī	52
narrate	叙	xù	134
narrow	窄	zhǎi	148
nauseated	恶	è	33
near	傍	bàng	3
neck	脖	bó	8
neck	领	lǐng	73
nervous	慌	huāng	50
night	夜	yè	138
not yet	未	wèi	124

nuclear	核	hé	47	pond	塘	táng	115
numerous	纷	fēn	36	pot	锅	guō	45
obedient	乖	guāi	43	pot	壶	hú	48
observe	遵	zūn	159	power	威	wēi	122
offer	献	xiàn	129	praise	赞	zàn	146
official	官	guān	43	precious thing	珍	zhēn	150
one another	彼	bǐ	5	prefecture	府	fǔ	38
one thousandth	厘	lí	69	pregnant	孕	yùn	146
only	唯	wéi	123	preserve	维	wéi	123
open	启	qǐ	92	prolong	延	yán	136
open	睁	zhēng	152	prominent	显	xiǎn	129
order	秩	zhì	154	protect	防	fáng	35
overcooked	烂	làn	67	provisions	粮	liáng	71
partner	伴	bàn	3	puff	喷	pēn	87
paternal aunt	姑	gū	41	punish	罚	fá	33
pattern	范	fàn	34	pure	纯	chún	21
peaceful	宁	nìng	84	purple	紫	zǐ	158
peach	桃	táo	116	pursue	逐	zhú	156
peak	顶	dǐng	29	pursue	追	zhuī	157
pear	梨	lí	69	put in order	措	cuò	23
pendulum	摆	bǎi	2	quarrel	吵	chǎo	15
penetrate	透	tòu	119	quiet	悄	qiāo	94
pepper	椒	jiāo	58	rabbit	兔	tù	121
personal	私	sī	111	rainbow	虹	hóng	47
pervade	彻	chè	15	raise	升	shēng	105
philosophy	哲	zhé	150	raised path	陌	mò	81
pick	采	cǎi	9	rank	阶	jiē	59
pick up	捡	jiǎn	56	rapid	迅	xùn	136
piece together	拼	pīn	89	rat	鼠	shǔ	110
pig	猪	zhū	155	rate	率	lǜ	74
pile	堆	duī	31	reach	达	dá	24
plain	素	sù	113	read aloud	念	niàn	84
plan	略	luè	75	reassure	慰	wèi	125
plan a project	企	qǐ	91	recommend	荐	jiàn	57
poem	诗	shī	106	record	录	lù	75
poison	毒	dú	31	reflect	映	yìng	141
politics	政	zhèng	152	regiment	团	tuán	121
pond	池	chí	17	register	版	bǎn	3

regret	憾	hàn	46
remit	汇	huì	51
repair	补	bǔ	8
represent	代	dài	24
reside	寓	yù	144
residence	舍	shè	103
respect	敬	jìng	60
respect	佩	pèi	87
respectful	恭	gōng	40
respectful	肃	sù	113
rest	歇	xiē	131
restore	恢	huī	51
retreat	退	tuì	121
return	返	fǎn	34
right	权	quán	96
rinse	冲	chōng	18
rise	涨	zhǎng	149
rock	石	shí	107
roll	卷	juǎn	62
room	屋	wū	126
root	源	yuán	144
rope	绳	shéng	105
rough	糙	cāo	11
rouse	振	zhèn	151
rub	摩	mó	81
rule	治	zhì	153
rush	闯	chuǎng	20
sad	悲	bēi	4
satirize	讽	fěng	37
sauce	酱	jiàng	57
saute	炒	chǎo	15
save	救	jiù	60
scald	烫	tàng	116
scatter	挥	huī	51
scatter	披	pī	88
scissors	剪	jiǎn	56
scold	骂	mà	76
search	搜	sōu	112

search	索	suǒ	114
search	寻	xún	135
second in order	乙	yǐ	139
secret	秘	mì	79
seem	佛	fú	37
seem	似	sì	112
send	致	zhì	154
separate	隔	gé	40
separate	析	xī	127
set up	设	shè	103
settled	稳	wěn	125
shake	摇	yáo	137
shake	震	zhèn	151
shake hands	握	wò	126
shallow	浅	qiǎn	92
share	股	gǔ	42
shield	盾	dùn	32
shoot	射	shè	103
shore	陆	lù	74
short of	乏	fá	33
shoulder	肩	jiān	55
side	测	cè	11
side room	厢	xiāng	130
silk	绸	chóu	19
silk	丝	sī	111
slanting	斜	xié	131
sleep	眠	mián	79
slippery	滑	huá	49
slow	缓	huǎn	50
sly	猾	huá	50
small net	络	luò	76
smart	俊	jùn	63
smear	涂	tú	120
smooth	润	rùn	99
snake	蛇	shé	102
sneeze	嚏	tì	117
soap	皂	zào	147
soft	柔	róu	98

soft	软	ruǎn	99
soldiers	兵	bīng	7
some	某	mǒu	82
speak of	谓	wèi	125
spear	矛	máo	77
spill	洒	sǎ	99
spirit	神	shén	104
sprout	苗	miáo	79
stage curtain	幕	mù	82
stand	立	lì	69
state	述	shù	110
stay	待	dài	25
stay idle	闲	xián	128
steal	偷	tōu	119
steamed bread	馒	mán	76
stench	臭	chòu	20
step upon	踩	cǎi	10
stick	贴	tiē	118
sticky	粘	zhān	148
still	尚	shàng	102
stomach	胃	wèi	124
strength	劲	jìn	60
stretch	伸	shēn	104
strong	强	qiáng	93
struggle	挣	zhèng	152
submerge	沉	chén	16
substitute for	替	tì	117
sudden	骤	zhòu	155
suddenly	忽	hū	48
sum up	综	zōng	158
sun	晒	shài	101
support	架	jià	55
support with hand	扶	fú	37
swear off	戒	jiè	59
tail	巴	bā	2
tail	尾	wěi	124
take a wife	娶	qǔ	96
tall building	厦	shà	100

tangerine	桔	jú	59
taxes	税	shuì	111
tear	撕	sī	111
tear open	拆	chāi	12
tears	泪	lèi	68
ten days	旬	xún	135
tender	嫩	nèn	83
thorn	刺	cì	22
threaten	胁	xié	132
throat	嗓	sǎng	100
throw	投	tóu	119
throw on ground	摔	shuāi	110
thunder	雷	léi	68
tide	潮	cháo	15
time	顿	dùn	32
toil	劳	láo	67
ton	吨	dūn	32
tooth	齿	chǐ	17
touch	碰	pèng	88
train	训	xùn	135
treat	疗	liáo	71
tree	木	mù	82
tremble	抖	dǒu	30
tribute	贡	gòng	40
unique	殊	shū	109
upper arm	膀	bǎng	3
urge	催	cuī	23
vegetables	蔬	shū	109
very large	巨	jù	61
victorious	胜	shèng	105
village	村	cūn	23
village	乡	xiāng	130
vinegar	醋	cù	22
virtue	德	dé	27
vomit	吐	tù	120
vulgar	俗	sú	112
waist	腰	yāo	137
wall	壁	bì	6

wall	墙	qiáng	94
warehouse	库	kù	64
water	浇	jiāo	58
way	途	tú	120
weak	弱	ruò	99
weary	疲	pí	88
weave	编	biān	6
weave	织	zhī	152
weigh	衡	héng	47
wheat	麦	mài	76
wheel	轮	lún	75
whip	鞭	biān	7
width	幅	fú	38
wing	翅	chì	18
wisdom	智	zhì	154
withdraw	缩	suō	114
woman	妇	fù	39
work out	制	zhì	153
worry about	愁	chóu	19
wound	创	chuàng	21
wrap around	裹	guǒ	45
yes	唉	ài	1
young	幼	yòu	142

27375223R00107

Made in the USA
Columbia, SC
23 September 2018